Communications in Computer and Information Science 1564

Imen Jemili · Mohamed Mosbah (Eds.)

Distributed Computing for Emerging Smart Networks

Third International Workshop, DiCES-N 2022
Bizerte, Tunisia, February 11, 2022
Proceedings

 Springer

Editors
Imen Jemili 🆔
University of Carthage
Zarzouna Bizerte, Tunisia

Mohamed Mosbah 🆔
University of Bordeaux
Bordeaux, France

ISSN 1865-0929   ISSN 1865-0937 (electronic)
Communications in Computer and Information Science
ISBN 978-3-030-99003-9   ISBN 978-3-030-99004-6 (eBook)
https://doi.org/10.1007/978-3-030-99004-6

This Springer imprint is published by the registered company Springer Nature Switzerland AG
The registered company address is: Gewerbestrasse 11, 6330 Cham, Switzerland

Preface

This volume contains the proceedings of the third Workshop in Distributed Computing for Emerging Smart Networks (DiCES-N 2022). The workshop was held on February 11, 2022, and took place virtually in order to ensure the safety of participants due to the COVID-19 pandemic. We received a total of 14 submissions, of which five were accepted for publication, and an invited paper. The acceptance rate was therefore approximately 35.7%. Reviewing was single-blind, where each paper was assigned to at least four reviewers.

Nowadays, the smart city concept is a rising vision of cities that seeks to enable broad connectivity and systems inter-operability and offer sustainable solutions and prevalent security. The smart cities are the nuclei from which smart networks and a new generation of solutions can be implemented to address their inherent challenges such as traffic congestion, air pollution, difficulty in waste management, scarcity of resources, and human health concerns. Smart cities rest on innovative paradigms and integrate new technologies into their infrastructures to enable their management and provide the basis for these innovative solutions. Smart living, smart mobility, smart people, smart environment, smart economy, and smart government are the main components of smart cities; these applications rely on the deployment of some sensing and tracking infrastructures for data collection from embedded sensors in smart devices, such as smart phones and connected cars. Thus, gathering data from the physical environment relies on a huge number of real-world physical entities, endowed with sensing, computation, and communication capabilities, and to some extent with some level of intelligence; this data will be forwarded, then stored, processed, and analyzed remotely to offer personalized services and support the proper functioning of these applications.

In this context, the Internet of Things (IoT), information and communication technologies (ICT), cloud computing and fog/edge computing are considered as key enabling technologies. In fact, IoT becomes a reality; a lot of applications in many domains rely on the new innovative IoT solutions. However, the fast-growing number of connected devices will require a new level of infrastructure deployment, both in terms of wired and wireless connectivity. Thus, the complex nature of IoT is reflected through the multitude of independent cyber-physical systems that operate with their own infrastructures and cooperate to achieve smart city sustainability through service reliability and security.

The workshop tackled issues relating to the design, development, and evaluation of distributed systems, platforms, and architectures for cyber-physical systems in the context of smart cities. The program included two sessions.

Session 1 was dedicated to emerging networks and communications, mainly wireless sensor networks (WSNs). In fact, the wide range of applications, potential uses, and great popularity of WSNs make them widely recognized as a major technology enabling the concept of smart cities. These networks are considered as the main sensing tool to collect contextual and environmental data and to observe real-world events, which will be exploited by upper-layer applications. This gathered data must be transmitted, shared, stored, and, finally, analyzed. This process requires the deployment of different technologies in each of these phases.

Designing the WSNs information life cycle in smart cities is a first step in understanding this complex process by identifying its phases and challenges, and the technologies involved. Thus, WSNs must coexist and collaborate with other networks, involving several technologies to support properly the functioning of the multiple smart applications. Depending on the application area, these networks may comprise a huge number of battery-operated sensor nodes, which are constrained in terms of energy and processing capabilities. Since it is imperative to keep such networks operative as long as possible, energy remains among the main issues. Replenishing the battery energy of the sensors can be difficult, expensive, or even impossible. Even the recourse to energy harvesting technology to capture energy from ambient power sources is costly and may be unaffordable for some applications. Moreover, communication through a wireless medium is inherently unreliable and is also prone to errors and link failures. Thus, the multiple challenges facing WSNs are related to the intrinsic characteristics of these networks and/or introduced by their large-scale deployment in the context of smart cities, as each smart application comes with its own challenges. Overcoming these issues is required as WSNs are a building block for data acquisition and innovative applications.

Session 1 covered the deployment of WSNs in smart farming applications and e-health. The recourse to WSNs in the field of agriculture has become a necessity for high added value and tangibility. Through smart agricultural applications, the optimization of agricultural production and resource utilization is targeted. Indeed, plants, trees, and shrubs can also suffer from insect infestations, diseases, and nutrient deficiencies. In addition, due to external factors, the losses to farming as a whole can be enormous. IoT is helping to overcome these challenges, mainly relating to extreme weather, climate change, and environmental impacts. With the introduction of IoT in agriculture, advanced sensors can be employed to collect data in real time, facilitating effective decision making.

The adoption of IoT has helped farmers in many activities such as monitoring water levels in reservoirs to increase the efficiency of the entire irrigation process and tracking seed growth. Indeed, smart farming applications allow the optimization of crop production and resource use. They cover a wide range of crop types monitored in diversified facilities, including greenhouse monitoring, vineyards, horticulture, and soil moisture monitoring in irrigation applications. However, the monitored field may extend over a large area, such as a greenhouse or a grassland, requiring the deployment of many sensors spread over the area. Thus, the sensor nodes need to cooperate to transmit the sensed data to a central node, called the sink node. The recourse to a routing protocol, suitable for the smart farming application, is essential to be able to deliver the data and commands correctly and in a timely manner; the automation process proposed by any smart farming application can exploit this information to achieve its objectives. Identifying the requirements of routing protocols in WSNs in the context of smart farming allows the selection of the most appropriate protocol for this application.

The suitability of a given protocol or technology depends mainly on the targeted application; the e-health domain was the second topic area discussed in Session 1 and wireless body area networks (WBANs) were introduced. WBANs are now widely deployed to provide effective and promising e-health solutions, such as ambulatory monitoring and assisted living at home. Indeed, technological advances have brought considerable and essential improvements to the health sector. Thank to biosensors, a patient's vital signs can be gathered around the clock and sent wirelessly to a mobile phone for self-remote monitoring or to a remote server for further analysis and storage. However, with the wide spread use of tablets, smartphones, and smartwatches and the integration of sensors in mobile devices, a huge amount of data is being collected. We rely on machine learning to deal with this large amount of data, which is beyond the capabilities of traditional data processing tools and techniques. By analyzing large volumes of data, machine-learning technology can assist healthcare professionals in generating accurate medical solutions tailored to individual characteristics.

Session 2 dealt with cyber security of connected devices. Despite the benefits brought by IoT, many issues remain unresolved and constitute a potential impediment to the uptake of IoT applications and the implementation of large-scale smart environments. Indeed, with the proliferation of smart devices and the rapid growth of high-speed networks, the Internet of Things has become an area of incredible impact and growth. The various connected smart devices, ranging from simple wearable accessories to large machines containing sensing chips, offer a panoply of services to facilitate the daily life of the citizen, ensure public safety, enhance public services, improve the productivity of companies, etc. These smart devices are starting to invade our lives; they collect a multitude of data relevant to services, in addition to contextual data that can improve data analysis and decision-making. However, this data can also be used to profile users and infiltrate their privacy. As IoT devices are easy to hack and compromise and are deployed in external and uncontrolled locations, new potential attack surfaces, that can be exploited by malicious cybercriminals, have emerged. In this context, traditional security solutions cannot be applied due to the intrinsic constraints of these intelligent systems and networks and their remarkable heterogeneity. Therefore, security has become one of the main concerns of this technology.

The manipulation of sensitive user information can lead to considerable damages, as in the field of e-health or intelligent transport. For instance, connected and self-driving cars present an attractive solution to major transport problems: improving road safety, alleviating traffic congestion, etc. To this end, vehicles will have to cooperate and exchange various information related to their position, behavior (deceleration, lane change, etc.), or the occurrence of external events (pedestrian, obstacle, etc.). However, to provide such safety-critical services, it is essential that communications between road users are secure. Healthcare applications also handle sensitive data related to patients; personal health data refers to a large range of information, including basic medical data (vital sign readings, patient status, and medical history), sensitive mental health data, or administrative data such as patient identity, address, etc. Due to the complexity of smart environments, preserving data privacy, confidentiality, and integrity is a challenging task. In this context, many emerging technologies have been employed to provide high-performance, privacy-friendly and secure architectures, such as the two tackled concepts, blockchain and software defined networking (SDN).

The key principle of blockchain rests on the notion of collective trust, without the intervention of a centralized trusted third party. Blockchain technology is a form of distributed ledger technology where each participant is responsible for the security of the network. This global and shared database is maintained among all these nodes, since each node in the network keeps all the transactions in the blockchain and participates in their verification and evolution. Once a transaction has been validated, no participant can sign or modify it. Thus, this distributed, synchronized, and duplicated ledger provides the same coherent, updated, and secure view to all participants in the network. Although this new system enables the exchange of data and money with low transaction costs and a privacy protection mechanism, it is relevant to identify the associated challenges and potential areas of application in different fields, such as e-health and vehicle networks as discussed in Session 2.

SDN also introduces many opportunities to protect the network more efficiently and flexibly, and to secure large-scale heterogeneous networks, by decoupling the data forwarding plane from the control plane. Thanks to the global view of a special node, called the SDN controller, such a node is able to provide network devices with the appropriate configuration, forwarding decisions, and security strategies. This functional behavior allows fast response to security threats, granular traffic filtering, and dynamic security policies. However, SDN can also come with its own security concerns. Indeed, through controllers, SDN enables centralized control and global visibility over the entire network. Even though a hybrid architecture involves multiple controllers, the failure of a single controller would put the entire network at risk; a component with malicious behavior can compromise the operation of the entire network. If the controllers in the network were attacked, the entire network would be paralyzed. In addition, threats to system vulnerabilities can affect the privacy, integrity, and confidentiality of the system, thus reducing the security, performance, and efficiency of the network. It is worthwhile to investigate the different threats against SDN and identify which part of the SDN paradigm they target and which aspects of security are affected, such as availability, integrity, and confidentiality.

We are grateful for the support provided by the many people who contributed to making DiCES-N 2022 success. Naturally, the workshop could not take place without the efforts made by the organizing committee who helped us to organize and publicize the event, particularly the Program Committee chairs (Sabra Mabrouk, Akka Zemmari, and Soumaya Dahi) and the publicity chair (Emna Ben Salem).

We are thankful to the members of the Programm Committee for providing their valuable time and helping us to review the received papers. We would also like to thank the authors for submitting and then revising a set of high-quality papers. Finally, we express our sincere gratitude to Springer for giving us the opportunity to publish the workshop proceedings, and we appreciate the support and advice provided by the editorial team.

February 2022

Imen Jemili
Mohamed Mosbah

Organization

General Chairs

Imen Jemili   University of Carthage, Tunisia
Mohamed Mosbah   Bordeaux INP, France

Program Committee Chairs

Sabra Mabrouk   University of Carthage, Tunisia
Soumaya Dahi   University of Carthage, Tunisia
Akka Zemmari   University of Bordeaux, France

Publicity Chair

Emna Ben Salem   University of Carthage, Tunisia

Program Committee

Salma Batti	University of Carthage, Tunisia
Raoudha Beltaifa	University of Manouba, Tunisia
Anis Ben Aicha	University of Carthage, Tunisia
Lotfi Ben Othmane	Iowa State University, USA
Ismail Berrada	Mohammed VI Polytechnic University, Morocco
Shridhar Devamane	TECSEC Technologies, India
Kamal E. Melkemi	University of Batna 2, Algeria
Ahmed El Oualkadi	Abdelmalek Essaâdi University, Morocco
Matthieu Gautier	University of Rennes 1, France
Tahani Gazdar	University of Jeddah, Saudi Arabia
Wilfried Yves Hamilton Adoni	Hassan II University of Casablanca, Morocco
Maha Jebalia	SUP'COM, Tunisia
Sondes Kallel	University of Paris-Saclay, France
Moez Krichen	Albaha University, Saudi Arabia
Hela Mahersia	University of Carthage, Tunisia
Bacem Mbarek	Masaryk University, Czech Republic
Nadhir Messai	University of Reims Champagne-Ardenne, France
Tarik Nahhal	Hassan II University of Casablanca, Morocco
Neha Pattan	Google, USA
Ashish Rauniyar	SINTEF Digital, Norway

Gautam Srivastava   Brandon University, Canada
Eiad Yafi   University of Kuala Lumpur, Malaysia
Anis Yazidi   Oslo Metropolitan University, Norway

Contents

Emerging Networks
and Communications

WSNs Information Life Cycle in the Context of Smart Cities

Chahrazed Ksouri[1,2,3(✉)] and Abdelfettah Belghith[4]

[1] Laboratoire DAVID, 45 Avenue des États Unis, 78000 Versailles, France
[2] Uni Bordeaux, CNRS, Bordeaux INP, LaBRI, UMR 5800, 33400 Talence, France
[3] National School of Engineers of Sfax, Sfax, Tunisia
chahrazedksouri@gmail.com
[4] College of Computer and Information Sciences, King Saud University, Riyadh, Saudi Arabia
abelghith@ksu.edu.sa

Abstract. Smart City concept is an emerging vision of cities with wide connectivity, systems inter-operability, sustainable solutions and prevalent security. Wireless Sensor Networks (WSNs) have shown themselves to be very useful in the process of the realization of this paradigm. Data collection is the first step on which the whole system is based. The new services and innovative applications offered by the Smart City are based on the extracted information from the data collected by sensors which are widely deployed and integrated in many smart devices such as smart phones and connected cars. In this paper, we introduce a WSNs information life cycle in Smart Cities encompassing six phases, namely; deployment, management, collect and transfer, use and share, storage, and analyses and plan. We specify for each phase the technologies involved. Then, we discuss the challenges of integration.

Keywords: Smart Cities · Wireless Sensor Networks · IoT · ICT · Big Data · Cloud Computing · SDN · FOG/EDGE Computing · UAV

1 Introduction

Technical, social, economic and organizational problems raised by the population growth and increased urbanization generate new challenges to be faced by cities such as traffic congestion, air pollution, difficulty in waste management, scarcity of resources and human health concerns [1]. During the last decade, with the emergence of new technologies and innovative paradigms such as IoT (Internet of Things) [2], ICT (Information and Communication Technologies) [3] and Cloud Computing [4], the trend is towards a vision of a Smart City, which maintains economic and environmental sustainability to provide better conditions of life to its citizens. Many Smart Cities initiatives have been launched all over the world, like in Seoul, Nelson Mandela Bay, Stockholm and Porto Alegre [5]. The

I. Jemili and M. Mosbah (Eds.): DiCES-N 2022, CCIS 1564, pp. 3–23, 2022.
https://doi.org/10.1007/978-3-030-99004-6_1

objectives pursued by these initiatives are different and depend on the cities conditions and needs. In Bangalore in India [6] where resources are limited, the coveted goal of the Smart City initiative is to achieve an acceptable standard of living for its citizens, while it targets a higher standard of living and it is based on much more resources in Dubai [7].

To achieve development over a wide geographic area and collect information from the physical world, the emerging concept of Smart City relies primarily on Wireless Sensor Networks and also on sensors embedded in devices that we use every day such as smart-phones, smart-watch, etc. WSN is a network made of sensors that perform service by sending signal or information periodically or whenever events occur [8]. In fact, wireless sensor networks are distributed systems composed of tiny autonomous nodes capable of sensing the environmental phenomena, such as temperature, pressure, vibration, humidity, vital signs and real word events [1]. These devices are characterized by:

- Limited battery: As WSNs do not rely on a fixed infrastructure and a centralized administration, the sensors must cooperate to assure network functionalities in a distributed manner. They must collaborate to forward collected data towards the sink in a multi-hop fashion and to ensure routing process and maintenance phase in case of route failure [9–12]. The failure of some nodes, due to power extinction, or the changing topology caused by node mobility can disturb the routing operation and the data forwarding.
- Low processing power: In fact, routing is considered as a challenging task in WSNs due to the limitation in energy and hardware capabilities of sensor nodes. Heavy and complex tasks must be avoided as sensors are characterized by limited internal resources in terms of memory and computational capacities, constraints to be considered with algorithmic complexity for the design of protocols at different stack levels, such as routing protocols [13]. Besides, the basic operations of a sensor node are sensing, data processing and communication, involving data transmission and reception. As these battery-powered nodes are usually deployed in remote or hard to reach areas, energy autonomy remains one of the main issues in the WSNs design.
- Short-range communication: Sensor nodes are characterized by limited bandwidth, imposed by the wireless shared medium. Sharing a wireless medium with neighboring nodes may result in eventual collisions and interference, which make communication unreliable [14]. Besides, due to the limited transmission range, sensor nodes perform data routing through multi-hop communication to reach the remote sink.

However, the potentialities of this networking paradigm, such as the low energy consumption, the easy deployment and the long life expectancy, make it an attractive option for providing user with new services and applications. In fact, WSNs are used in many industrial and civilian applications collecting all kinds of data ranging from scalar to multimedia traffic. However, exploiting these networks at a large scale comes with a number of challenges, inherent to WSNs or introduced when deployed in the context of Smart Cities. Ensuring QoS (Quality of Service) requirements for the well functioning of proposed services and avoiding any failure or service disrupt causing dissatisfaction and inconvenience to the user is one of the main faced challenges.

Only a few works surveyed the use of WSNs in Smart Cities such as the work proposed in [15] and [16]. The authors, in [15], gave some examples of WSNs applications in smart homes and cities namely energy-saving applications, noise and atmospheric monitoring and healthcare monitoring. This work also highlighted some challenges faced by WSNs in the context of Smart Cities such as access technologies, routing strategies, power-saving methods and security. In [16], authors focused on node deployment and sensing management of WSNs for Smart City monitoring. They provided a comprehensive understanding and sound design guidelines enabling to choose the existing algorithms in different type of monitoring applications such as structural health monitoring, water pipeline networks, camera sensor network, traffic monitoring, smart grid monitoring, streetlight monitoring.

To the best of our knowledge, this work represents the first attempt proposing a WSNs information life cycle in the context of Smart Cities while specifying technological integrations. The key contributions of this paper are as follows:

- We propose a WSNs information life cycle focusing on the integration with several technologies involved in the Smart City concept. The proposal encompasses six steps, namely deployment, management, collect and transfer, use and share, storage, analyses and plan. This will be useful for academia and industry researchers to acquire a holistic vision regarding the deployment of WSNs in the Smart Cities.
- We point out the challenges that hinder the full technological integration of the WSNs paradigm in the context of Smart Cities, which will help to propose better WSN-based solutions for Smart Cities considering the limitations of integrations.

The remainder of the paper is structured as follows. In Sect. 2, we introduce the life cycle of WSNs information when deployed in Smart Cities, while specifying for each phase the technologies involved. In Sect. 3, we present the challenges related to the technological integration at each phase. We conclude this paper, in Sect. 4.

2 WSNs Information Life Cycle in Smart Cities

The fields of Smart City are diverse ranging from environment, people, governance, economy, life and mobility[1,17,18]. The concept rests on Cyber-Physical Systems (CPS) to control physical devices in order to sense the environment and modify it [19]. According to [20], a cyber-physical system is *"a system including a strict coordination between, and, combination of the physical and computational elements of system"*. In CPSs, Wireless Sensor Networks have a prominent role as Sensor Based Systems (SBS) [20] to allow recognition of the physical world by the computational part of the system. These networks have to cohabit and collaborate with other networks, involving several technologies to ensure the functioning of the Smart City. In fact, Smart Cities leaders rely on information processed by the intelligent subsystems to make the best decisions and ensure ecosystem harmonization while maintaining the goal of making the city more economically and environmentally attractive. Before being able to exploit such information, data must be collected, then forwarded, shared, stored and finally, analysed. This process requires the involvement of different technologies at each of these phases. We made our proposition based on both WSN networks handling tasks such as deployment and management and the different tasks performed on data namely collect, transfer, analyse, etc. As exposed in Fig. 1, we illustrate the life cycle of WSNs information in Smart Cities. The first four steps; deployment, management, collect and transfer, and use and share focus on WSNs. And the three last ones; storage, analyses and plan concern the collected data.

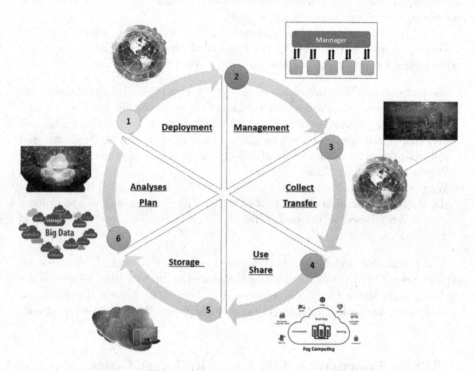

Fig. 1. WSNs information life cycle in Smart Cities

In the following sub sections, we detail the life cycle of the information collected by WSNs in the Smart Cities. We will introduce each phase while highlighting the involved technologies.

2.1 Deployment

The deployment of the Wireless Sensor Networks represents the first step in WSNs-based solutions development. When deploying WSNs, several parameters must be taken into consideration namely: deployment cost, coverage, connectivity, sensors reliability, network lifetime and deployment conditions [21]. Two ways are feasible for the deployment according to the application and to its target environment [21]. The first one is the pre-determined deployment, where a specific position is assigned to each single node. Many applications adopt this model, such as video surveillance. The second scheme is the random technique, used when sensor nodes are deployed on hostile environments or in large-scale open regions. Forest fire detection [22], monitoring earthquake and volcanic activities [22] are examples of applications requiring such kind of deployment. In this context, UAV (Unmanned Aerial Vehicle, see Fig. 2) systems were proposed in many solutions [23,24] to support WSNs in the different phases of their deployment, especially when WSNs are utilized in hostile and unreachable environments, such as volcano, desert and some dense forests, as depicted in Fig. 3. In fact, an Unmanned Aerial Vehicle is an aircraft without a human pilot aboard. The flight of UAVs may operate with various degrees of autonomy, either under remote control by a human operator or autonomously by on-board computer [25]. Thus, UAV presents a good solution to deploy the sensor nodes on such places by dropping them on attended/unattended way [23].

Fig. 2. Unmanned Aerial Vehicle.

2.2 Management

The management of WSN consists of the definition of a set of functions to promote productivity and to integrate the configuration, the operation, the administration and the maintenance of the WSN components and services [26]. Management solutions have to consider the characteristics of WSNs, such as, the restricted physical resources: energy and computational capabilities, recovery from node failure, data acquisition accuracy/redundancy and security threats.

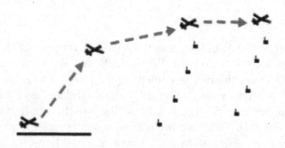

Fig. 3. UAVs deploying WSN [23].

Once the Wireless Sensor Network is deployed, its elements cooperate to route the collected data in a distributed manner. In fact, each node has to identify its neighbors that will be in charge of relaying the data toward the sink. In addition, in the case of the extinction of a node caused by a dysfunction or a discharge of the battery, the network elements need to restore the paths to the sink bypassing the defective node. To perform these tasks: sensing, communication, routing and data processing, the nodes must draw on their limited resources, which impacts the life span of the network. These last years, novel network architecture models integration new paradigm, such as Software Defined Network (SDN), have emerged to handle some of the mentioned tasks and expand the lifetime of the WSN networks [27].

The adoption of SDN approach to manage WSNs seems to offer promising opportunities for increasing their efficiency. The SDN is a new approach to construct and manage the network architecture in which the layers of administration, control and data transfer are separated [28]. Figure 4 presents the architecture of Software Defined Wireless Sensor Networks (SDWSN) [29]. Operations such as; topology discovery, routing selection, information collection are shifted/processed at the control plans. The communication between these layers is carried out through Application Programming Interfaces (APIs): northbound APIs for application-control plans communication and southbound APIs for controller-data plans communication.

Table 1 presents a comparison of different SDWSNs proposed architectures. The classification criteria are the ability of models to handle configuration, scalability and energy efficiency.

The objective of the concept is not restricted to the decoupling of the plans. Indeed, SDN is considered as an architecture to open the network to applications by enabling an automated programmability. In fact, in a Smart City context where hundreds of thousands of heterogeneous sensor nodes are deployed over IoT, the main difficulty is the lack of optimal management of such large and heterogeneous networks in order to allow ubiquitous access to the data gathered. The SDN-based management for WSNs is envisaged to potentially solve most of the inherent WSN challenges [34,35], in addition to some related to its deployment in Smart Cities:

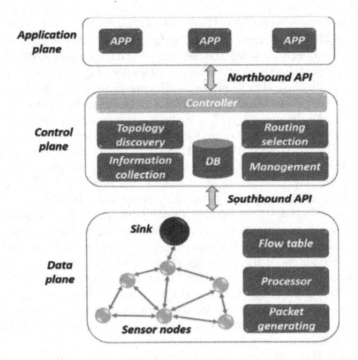

Fig. 4. The basic SDWSN framework [29].

Table 1. SDN-based WSN architectures

SDWSN	Controller Configuration	Configuration	Scalability	Energy Efficiency
Sensor OpenFlow [30]	Distributed	yes	no	no
Smart [31]	Centralized	no	yes	yes
TinySDN [32]	Distributed	no	yes	no
SDWN [33]	Centralized	yes	no	yes

- Network management and configuration: The decoupling of the control and data plans will reduce the burden of reconfiguration and maintenance on the constrained-capabilities nodes. They will be simple forwarding elements, while the controller in the upper plane will handle control logic [34]. Moreover, thanks to the flexibility property of the SDN model, tasks such as the employment of new routing protocols will go without re-configuring the nodes, as required by classical networks [35].
- Routing, Mobility and Localization: Traditional routing protocols are energy intensive process. In fact, they rely on the cooperation between the constrained-nodes to take routing decisions in both proactive and reactive schemes. In addition, their convergence time is affected by sensors mobility and the nodes localization accuracy. In SDN-based models, controllers

handle the management of policies and routing decisions [31]. Furthermore, the possibility to administrate the nodes mobility and localization by the central controller may lower the convergence time. As suggested in [31], the controller can keep track of nodes' locations by receiving updates on their moves. Localization algorithms for SDSNs are proposed in [36,37].

- Energy: Energy consumption represents one of the main factors to take into account while developing WSNs. Reducing the energy consumed by nodes will save power and therefore prolong the network life span. To achieve such purpose, the SDN-based WSNs [31,38] shift certain energy intensive functions usually performed by the network nodes to the SDN controller [39]. For example, routing function, in point of fact, the nodes will only execute the instructions assigned by the controller to route data. In addition, according to [33], SDN-based WSNs solution should support traditional strategies for limiting energy consumption such as duty cycles and in-network data aggregation. Several energy preservation-oriented SDN solutions was proposed for Wireless Sensor Networks. An adaptation of the sleep scheduling mechanism to SDN-based WSNs is presented in [40]. In [41] a concept of layer head is proposed, where a LH (Layer Head) is elected based on the energy criterion and it is in charge of sanding the information to the controller. An energy-efficient algorithm based on multi-dimensional energy space for software-defined wireless sensor networks is presented in [42].

- Scalability: Managing scalability represents one of the main drawbacks of the large scale deployment of WSN technology in Smart Cities. With the global view acquired by the SDWSN controller upon the network and the high-level abstractions, the scalability became a less complex task, especially, with the distributed controllers configuration [32,43–45] that enhance the centralized ones [31,33], by ensuring network performance and availability, in addition to scalability.

- Interoperability: In the context of Smart Cities, the lack of interoperability among the involved subsystems slows its realization. Alleviating the dependency in term of hardware and software of the heterogeneous infrastructure elements by mean of the high-level abstractions and the decentralized control offered by SDN approaches [30] will permit a perfect interoperability among multi-vendors and multi-devices networks.

- Security: From a security point of view, the SDN-network elements devoid of intelligence represent a passive defense line in the face of malicious actions. In fact, it would be insignificant to conduct attacks from such dump element which only understand and execute the controller commands [34]. Furthermore, SDN can also ensure the security of the system by avoiding the vulnerabilities generated by manual configuration errors.

2.3   Collect and Transfer

Data gathering is the primary functionality of a WSN network. Depending on the application need and sensor nodes types, the collected data can be heterogeneous and have different QoS requirements [46]. Different physical quantities are measured [47] such as angle, magnetic field, debit, displacement, distance (optical, ultrasound, microwave), strength, light (photodiode or phototransistor, photographic sensor, photoelectric cell), level (gamma ray, ultrasound, by radar), position, sound (microphone, hydrophone), pressure (barometer, hypsometric), temperature (thermometer, thermistor) and video WSNs. As sensors are powered by limited batteries, energy remains the most critical resource for WSNs. Once the energy is exhausted, the whole network may be partitioned into disjoint sub-networks; in such situation, some readings cannot be sent to any sink [48]. In the Smart Cities context, the large-scale deployment of WSNs imposes the nodes collaboration in order to forward collected data towards the sink, which increases the energy consumption.

In Table 2, we present the different wireless communication technologies available for WSNs:

UAV technology is also employed to collect the data gathered by WSNs [49,50]. This approach considers the UAV entity as a mobile sink [49]. Unlike the solution focusing on the one-to-one data collection scheme, where a UAV can collect the sensing data from one sensor at each time, authors in [50] proposed a solution adopting the one-to-many data collection scheme. In fact, the UAV can collect sensing data from multiple sensors simultaneously through the Orthogonal Frequency Division Multiple Access (FDMA) technique. Such a solution enables to maximize the volume of data collected in less hovering duration of the UAV, thus considering the energy capacity constraint of the UAV [50].

Table 2. WSNs communication technologies

	IEEE 802.15.4				UWB	Bluetooth	BLE	Z-wave	ANT	Wavenis	Dash7	EnOcean
	ZigBee	6LoWPAN	WirelessHART	ISA100.11a								
Frequency	868/915 MHz; 2.4 GHz				3.1–10.6 GHz	2.4 GHz	2.4 GHz	sub-1 GHz	2.4 GHz	868, 915, 433 MHz	433 MHz	868; 315 MHz
Data rate	250 kbps				110 Mbps	3 Mbps	1 Mbps	40 kbps	1 Mbps	100 kbps	200 kbps	125 kbps
Range	10–100	1–100	1–100	100	10	10–100	200	30		1–4	2	300
Power consumption	Very low	Low	Low	Low	Low	Low	Ultra low	Low	Ultra low	Ultra low	Low	Ultra low

2.4   Use and Share

Once the data is gathered, two options might be considered besides the sending of the data to the Cloud. This depends on the application for which this data is collected and the WSN nature. First, the WSN includes actuators, so actions must be undertaken upon the reception of the data for example in fire detection application, in addition to the alarm initiation, the fire safety system must be launched. Second, the data collected by one application can be used by another. We take the example of a WSN deployed near highways by a weather applications, the collected data can be routed to the road infrastructure to serve the weather condition alert applications in the case of frost.

However, to decide for the use and the share of this gathered data an intelligence must be introduced near to the edge of the network, this is where the Fog and Edge technologies come in. We have to mention that the utilization of these technologies will not substitute in an integral way the functions provided by the Cloud at the Smart City scale. In fact, functions such as, processing operation that have to be done at the edge of the network for delay and QoS reasons and temporary storage, will benefit from the technologies utilities. However, functions that necessitate a global vision, such as decision-making, will take place at the Cloud level so on for the storage of statistics and shared data. Some works address the integration of Fog Computing with WSNs [51–53]. Qussai et al. [51] proposed a model leveraging the infrastructure of Fog Computing to address the major issues of intrusions detection, such as selective forwarding, in mobile WSNs. The model provides a global monitoring capability for tracing moving sensors and detecting malicious ones. In the work presented in [52], FOGG (Fog Computing Based Gateway) was proposed in order to integrate various heterogeneous sensor networks with the Internet to realize IoT. FOGG uses a dedicated device to function as an IoT gateway. It provides the needed integration along with additional services like name/protocol translation, security and controller functionalities. Authors in [53], proposed an innovative platform enhancing IWSN (Industrial Wireless Sensor Networks) architectures by adding a processing layer at the network edge. The proposed system exploits the Fog computing paradigm to design a sensing board to monitor different operating parameters of an asynchronous electric motor.

2.5   Storage

After the mining and the extraction of the value information from the data and their utilization, there are several reasons for keeping some specific data like the one that can be used on future research or for historical and statistic purposes. In the distributed large-scale WSNs where heterogeneous applications generating hundreds of thousands of gigabytes of structured, unstructured, binary and multimedia data, the managing of the data must be delegate to another entity in view of the limitation of the technology constituents in terms of energy, processing and memory capabilities. Given that, the current technologies are not able to provide sufficient data storage, Cloud Computing seems to be the most adequate solution with its virtually infinite capacity for data storage [54]. The interaction between WSNs and Cloud Computing technology is based on the shift of data from the WSNs into the Cloud environment. This will help to have a more effective management of the generated data to reach a fully exploitation of the scientifically valuable information.

The concept of the Cloud Computing technology is based on making a set of expensive, available only for a few, and technically challenging tasks, such as powerful computational tools and storage resources accessible for everyone by making almost everything dematerialized [55]. In fact, the technology allows delivering on-demand resources and services over the Internet with maximum performance [55]. There are different categories of services provided by Cloud Computing; Infrastructure as a Service (IaaS) [54], Platform as a Service (PaaS)

[54], Service as a Service (SaaS) [56], and more recently Big Data as a Service (BDaaS) [57] and Hadoop as a Service (HaaS) [4].

As the Cloud Computing provides applications, platforms and infrastructure over the Internet, this means the data generated by WSNs will be shift to an environment where it can be stored, processed and queried into/through it. The involvement of the Cloud will take part from the phase, which follows the gathering and transmission of the data until its final delivery to the users. In fact, the Cloud presents enormous capabilities for data storage, and when it comes to the data processing, the technology offers a scalable computing abilities, while for the final step, which is the presentation to the end-users, Cloud integrates an agile applications development tools [3]. This cohesive programming platform contributes in the unification of the underlying ecosystems by allowing interaction between the different applications in a common environment, thus allowing a more fluid and secure exchange of their collected data. Furthermore, Cloud allows an effective utilization of the WSNs by making it available for several applications and saving coast. Moreover, if the applications are depending from a unified environment, the development of a unique interface for interacting with the different applications will save time spent on APIs conceiving.

Figure 5 presents the architecture of Edge, Fog and Cloud Computing [58]:

2.6 Analyses and Plan

Sensor nodes are playing an important role on supplying concerned parts such as monitoring and control applications with data on the city scale. In addition to the recent development of information and communication technologies, an explosion in the volume of data generated by WSNs has emerged. All the extracted valuable information from WSNs gathered data will be in the hands of the leaders. They will be able to make more relevant decisions based on this information. By the adoption of the Big Data concept to manage the data generated on the Smart Cities, WSNs are considered as the major providers of these systems with the data.

The data generated by WSNs is managed in a centralized way. In fact, all the readings are routed by the sensor nodes to the sinks and then to the corresponding data center where the data will be stored and processed. In Smart City context the amounts of connected objects is enormous, Big Data system represents the adequate solution to manage this type of data which is characterized by its enormous amount, it's continuous generation and it's heterogeneous sources, which satisfies the main 3 Vs criteria of Big Data which are Volume, Velocity and Variety [59].

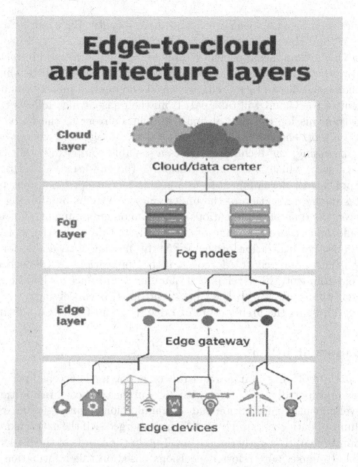

Fig. 5. Edge-to-Cloud architecture layers [58].

Big Data represents both a term describing the exponentially growing data with different kinds (structured, unstructured, semi-structured) and coming from heterogeneous sources, and a paradigm that encompasses mechanisms of collecting, storing, handling and extracting meaning from this data, which exceeds the processing capabilities of traditional databases [60].

A dedicated Big Data infrastructure for analysing data generated by Wireless Sensor Networks was designed in [61]. The proposed infrastructure enables to monitors (processing and storage) data generated by a WSN about air pollution at a city level. Secure both data capture and transport performed at the WSN level is an important task [62]. Several work were proposed to secure these phases in WSNs integrating Big Data systems [63,64].

3   Discussion

As presented in the previous subsection, throughout their deployment WSNs are coupled with other technologies fostering their adaptation to the Smart City context. However, despite the great potential of these integrations, many challenges must be addressed in order to reach their optimal effectiveness. We discuss in what follows the challenges at the different phases of WSNs deployment:

- In Smart City environment, WSNs are an integrated part of IoT concept that allows ubiquitous access to information collected through different technological platforms. IoT paradigm from a functional point of view represents a conceptualization of the physical world by connecting its embedded devices to interact with them in order to collect data and submit them actions to accomplish. In such context, the major problem related to WSNs deployment by IoT concept lies on the fact that it has to be connected to the Internet [65]. In fact, the transmission of collected data via Internet will add an extra layer of security issues [66], since the data may be intercepted by a third party at any time during its transmission through the network. In addition to the possibility of manipulating the sensor nodes by infiltrating orders from an intruder. Besides, in IoT systems, every connected device is either a data source or/and an actuator, in both cases, an identification of the entity is mandatory. First, the source identification is essential for traceability reasons required by some applications and it is a guarantee for the transparency of the technology functioning. In fact, knowing details such as the origin and time of data release creates a climate of trust and allows a better management of safety. Secondly, the identification of the actuator is needed to manage and address him remotely; thus, it will be able to receive remote orders from the ecosystem. Being an intrinsic part of the IoT implies that the constrained-resources nodes of WSNs must be identified. Several integration approaches were proposed to successfully integrate WSN in the Internet [65]. Table 3 presents the different existing approaches for WSNs integration in the IoT:
- The management of WSNs using SDN networking paradigm offers many advantages at the different levels namely management, configuration, routing, mobility, localization, energy, scalability, interoperability and security. The integration of WSN networking paradigms within Wireless Sensors Networks may present some risks [29,67]:
  - As seen in previous sections SDN-based management architecture for WSNs can be either centralized [31,33] or distributed [30,32]. The main weakness of the first one is the single point of failure problem, as the network will be paralysed if the controller is out of service. The control messages exchange is the weak point of the second approach. In fact, this burden the network and shorten the network life time.

Table 3. WSNs integration approaches

Solutions	Description	Benefits	Limitations
TCP/IP	• Sensors implement the TCP/IP stack • Considered as full-fledged elements	Direct access to the device	External attacks
Gateway	The gateway route the information	Store and forward, redundancy	Single point of failure
Front-end	Sensors implement their own set of protocols	Application-layer access	Single point of failure

- The SDN system implemented in the constrained capacity and energy sensor nodes could consume a lot of power, thus threatening the life' of the network [29].
- Another important issue is the level of intelligence of the network nodes. In fact, there are several programming models for SDN allowing nodes to acquire a certain level of intelligence [67]. If the elements of the network are simply executors of the controller consigns without any processing autonomy, several problems will arise. For instance, as the WSN is solely dependent on controllers, in case of an attack or a communication failure, the network will be defenseless and devoid of intelligence to act. In addition, it would be difficult to reduce data redundancy, save energy and optimize bandwidth use, made feasible by performing data aggregation or decision fusion at the data plan.

- ICT, Information and Communications Technologies, is a term that encompasses the set of infrastructure, devices, networking components, applications and systems of those various components, that combined allow the interaction with the digital world. For WSNs, ICTs provide the means of communication between the components of the network in order to carry the gathered data to other parts of the ecosystem, which are responsible of decision-making and services delivery. The major challenges facing ICTs are:
  - Network Bandwidth: With the technological advancements, the data detected by the WSN networks acquire multidimensional characteristics brought by their heterogeneous sources, format, etc. The gathered data rang from physical dimensions (temperature, pressure, flow, speed, etc.) to multimedia content (streaming video, voice and images with real-time needs). The challenges lies, at the first time, on the consideration of the constrained sensor node to be able to handle the processing and exchange of this type of data. At the second times the challenge resides in the accurate transfer of a such huge volume of data in a timely manner using conventional networks, e.g., mobile, WLAN, MAN and ADSL [3].
  - Wireless channels: Due to the open property of wireless channels, conflicts will happen in time, space or frequency dimension when the channel is

shared among multiple components [68]. With the large-scale deployment of WSNs at a city wide dimensions the problem will increase due to the density of networks and the coexistence of other wireless communication such as mobile network. The function of access network technologies is to manage and coordinate the use of channels resources to ensure the interconnection and communication of multiple users on the shared channel. The integration of security mechanisms within the protocols taking into account the specificity of the different applications is needed.

– WSNs deployed across a city employ different protocols and gather different formats of data and this represents a problem at the level of Fog Computing [69]. In fact, the traditional approaches for data acquisition and normalization implemented in the Cloud, are not well-suited in resource-constrained Fog [70]. The use of Fog enables to reduce traffic overhead leveraging storage and computing services toward edge devices. However, how to decide which data should go to Cloud or be processed in Fog level represents a concern [71].

– WSNs generated data will be shifted to the Cloud, which provides applications, platforms and infrastructure over the Internet, environment where it can be stored, processed and queried into/through it. Despite the fact that the Cloud Computing meets the different requirements of the large deployment of WSNs, a further study ensuring a more efficient integration between these two technologies is needed:

  • Several energy-efficient techniques were proposed to extend the network life time, thus enabling more efficient WSNs Cloud-based use. However, more work is needed to ensure QoS-related requirements such as reliability, availability, throughput, deadline, and accuracy [72].

  • Security and privacy are major concerns for WSNs integrating Cloud, especially for sensitive data such as the one issued from healthcare applications like body sensor network [73]. Security mechanisms must be implemented to ensure the integrity and confidentiality of the system at all deployment stages [74].

  • One other major challenge is that the poor communication ability of WSNs represent a bottleneck for the data delivery process from WSNs to Cloud. Since sensors are with low bandwidth and low energy supplies, it is difficult to meet the requirement of real-time data delivery from WSNs to Cloud [72].

– The function of management ensured by the Big Data system encompasses tasks of analysis, processing and querying of the data. To ensure effective functioning of these different tasks, measures must be taken accompanying the data until it is delivered to end users who may be applications or people. In this perspective, several challenges will be encountered on two major levels:

  • Analyses level: The data coming from the sensor network are unstructured, voluminous and derived from heterogeneous sources which make their analysis by the classic methods difficult and new techniques of mining which take into account the data characteristics are needed. In fact, as mentioned on the previous section traditional data mining tools aren't equipped to parse unstructured data and to do so all of this information would be converted into structured data however, this would be costly and time consuming [75], especially in Smart Cities context where the data arrived in large volumes and mixed form. As Smart Cities introduce themselves as answers to the quest for more responsive cities, which reacts effectively in the briefest delay to face the challenges bring by today's urban live, real-time analyses of some of the generated data must be executed instantaneously. This represent a major challenge to be faced by the researchers that attempt to combine WSNs and Big Data technologies.

- Query processing level: Once organized and stored, the data have to be retrieved from the databases. This action can be proceed either by a user through an interface proposed by the stockholders of the city such as (parking place, etc.) or an application (monitoring physical and environmental changes such as temperature and pressure, disasters control, etc.) to extract values from the data. Moreover, in the study of the Smart City evolution, creating behavior pattern of some systems such mobility is needed. In these cases, the data to analyse had to be stored for periods up to 6 months, which represents an enormous amount of data to handle. The classic query engines were dedicated to structured data with small volume which is not the current case, the challenges lies on the need of new query processing mechanisms to ensure these actions, to make the retrieve of this unstructured data possible and fluid.

The employed technologies, their integration objectives and challenges are summarized in Table 4:

Table 4. WSNs applications in smart environment domain

	Technologies	Integration objective	Challenges
Deployment	UAV	• Deployment of the WSN nodes in harsh environment and inaccessible spots	• Hovering duration
	ICT	• Integration into the IoT system	• Security vulnerabilities
Managing	SDN	• Network management and configuration	• Centralized controller: Single point of failure for
		• Routing	• Distributed controller: Burden the network with control messages
		• Energy	• Energy greedy
		• Scalability	
		• Interoperability	
		• Security	
Collect & transfer	ICT	• Inter WSNs communications	• Network bandwidth
		• Intra WSNs communications	• Wireless channel
	UAV	• Mobile sink	• Hovering duration
Use & share	Edge-fog computing	• Temporary store	• Different protocols handling
		• Real-time response	• Several data types formats
Storage	Cloud computing	• Storage	• QoS requirements
		• Security	• Security and privacy
		• Organization	
Analyse & plan	Bid data	• Data analysis	• Query process
		• Data processing	• Real time applications
		• Data querying	

4   Conclusion

Potential applications of Smart Cities are diverse, permeating into practically all areas of every-day life of individuals, enterprises, and society as a whole. Though this work, we proposed a WSNs information life cycle in the context of Smart Cities discussing the integration of WSNs with different technologies in term of benefits and challenges. These integrations are mainly targeted to solve task such network management, handling heterogeneous-node networks to support concurrent and diverse applications while tackling variation in area covered, required capacity and the non-uniformity of node distribution, scalability issues and the interoperability of multiple communication technologies. The involvement of multiple stakeholders in the process of data gathering, handling, processing, analysing and storing, arises security and privacy issues and induces the development of mechanisms to guarantee the basic security requirements for real-time and secure data communication, protection of data and measurements, data integrity and confidentiality. In future work, we would like to review the main WSN based applications in Smart Cities and to investigate the challenges facing their large-scale deployment.

References

1. Chourabi, H., et al.: Understanding smart cities: an integrative framework. In: 2012 45th Hawaii International Conference on System Sciences, pp. 2289–2297. IEEE (2012)
2. 16bn devices online by 2020. http://www.telegraph.co.uk/technology/internet/-8097488/16bn-devices-online-by-2020-says-report.html. Accessed Sept 2021
3. Liu, R., Wassell, I.J.: Opportunities and challenges of wireless sensor networks using cloud services. In: Proceedings of the Workshop on Internet of Things and Service Platforms, p. 4. ACM (2011)
4. HaaS. http://searchstorage.techtarget.com/definition/hadoop-as-a-service-haas. Accessed Sept 2021
5. Nam, T., Pardo, T.A.: Conceptualizing smart city with dimensions of technology, people, and institutions. In: Proceedings of the 12th Annual International Digital Government Research Conference: Digital Government Innovation in Challenging Times, pp. 282–291. ACM (2011)
6. 5gaa. https://5gaa.org/5g-technology/paving-the-way/. Accessed Sept 2021
7. Dassani, N., Nirwan, D., Hariharan, G.: Dubai-A New Paradigm for Smart Cities. KPMG International Dubai (2015)
8. Begum, K., Dixit, S.: Industrial WSN using IOT: a survey. In: 2016 International Conference on Electrical, Electronics, and Optimization Techniques (ICEEOT), pp. 499–504. IEEE (2016)
9. Ghrab, D., Jemili, I., Belghith, A., Mosbah, M.: Ndrect: node-disjoint routes establishment for critical traffic in WSNs. In: 2016 International Wireless Communications and Mobile Computing Conference (IWCMC), pp. 702–707. IEEE (2016)
10. Jemili, I., Tekaya, G., Belghith, A.: A fast multipath routing protocol for wireless sensor networks. In: 2014 IEEE/ACS 11th International Conference on Computer Systems and Applications (AICCSA), pp. 747–754. IEEE (2014)

11. Jemili, I., Ghrab, D., Belghith, A., Mosbah, M.: Cross-layer adaptive multipath routing for multimedia wireless sensor networks under duty cycle mode. Ad Hoc Netw. **109**, 102292 (2020)
12. Jemili, I., Ghrab, D., Belghith, A., Mosbah, M., Al-Ahmadi, S.: Cross-layer multipath approach for critical traffic in duty-cycled wireless sensor networks. J. Netw. Comput. Appl. **191**, 103154 (2021)
13. Jemili, I., Tekaya, G., Belghith, A.: A fast multipath routing protocol for wireless sensor networks. In: 2014 IEEE/ACS 11th International Conference on Computer Systems and Applications (AICCSA), pp. 747–754 (2014)
14. Ghrab, Dhouha, Jemili, Imen, Belghith, Abdelfettah, Mosbah, Mohamed: Correlation-Free MultiPath Routing for Multimedia Traffic in Wireless Sensor Networks. In: Puliafito, Antonio, Bruneo, Dario, Distefano, Salvatore, Longo, Francesco (eds.) ADHOC-NOW 2017. LNCS, vol. 10517, pp. 276–289. Springer, Cham (2017). https://doi.org/10.1007/978-3-319-67910-5_23
15. Belghith, A., Obaidat, M.S.: Wireless sensor networks applications to smart homes and cities. In: Smart Cities and Homes, pp. 17–40. Elsevier (2016)
16. Du, R., Santi, P., Xiao, M., Vasilakos, A.V., Fischione, C.: The Sensable City: A Survey on the Deployment and Management for Smart City Monitoring, vol. 21, pp. 1533–1560. IEEE (2018)
17. Ksouri, C., Jemili, I., Mosbah, M., Belghith, A.: A unified smart mobility system integrating terrestrial, aerial and marine intelligent vehicles. In: International Workshop on Communication Technologies for Vehicles, pp. 203–214. Springer, Cham (2020). https://doi.org/10.1007/978-3-030-66030-7_18
18. Ksouri, C.: Smart Mobility and Routing in Intermittent Infrastructure-Based Internet of Vehicles. PhD thesis, Université de Bordeaux; Université de Sfax (Tunisie) (2020)
19. IBM. https://developer.ibm.com/articles/ba-cyber-physical-systems-and-smart-cities-iot/. Accessed Sept 2021
20. Giraldo, J., Sarkar, E., Cardenas, A.A., Maniatakos, M., Kantarcioglu, M.: Security and privacy in cyber-physical systems: a survey of surveys. IEEE Design Test **34**(4), 7–17 (2017)
21. Senouci, M.R., Mellouk, A.: Deploying Wireless Sensor Networks: Theory and Practice. Elsevier (2016)
22. Vermesan, O., Friess, P.: Internet of Things: Converging Technologies for Smart Environments and Integrated Ecosystems. River Publishers (2013)
23. Tuna, G., Mumcu, T.V., Gulez, K., Gungor, V.C., Erturk, H.: Unmanned aerial vehicle-aided wireless sensor network deployment system for post-disaster monitoring. In: Huang, D.-S., Gupta, P., Zhang, X., Premaratne, P. (eds.) ICIC 2012. CCIS, vol. 304, pp. 298–305. Springer, Heidelberg (2012). https://doi.org/10.1007/978-3-642-31837-5_44
24. Sørli, J.-V., Graven, O.H.: Multi-drone framework for cooperative deployment of dynamic wireless sensor networks. In: Tan, Y., Shi, Y., Tang, Q. (eds.) ICSI 2018. LNCS, vol. 10942, pp. 74–85. Springer, Cham (2018). https://doi.org/10.1007/978-3-319-93818-9_8
25. ICAO's Circular 328 AN/190: Unmanned Aircraft Systems. http://www.icao.int/meetings/uas/documents/circular. Accessed Sept 2021
26. Ruiz, L.B., Nogueira, J.M., Loureiro, A.A.F.: Manna: a management architecture for wireless sensor networks. IEEE Commun. Magaz. **41**(2), 116–125 (2003)
27. Rbii, E., Jemili, I.: Leveraging SDN for smart city applications support. In: Jemili, I., Mosbah, M. (eds.) DiCES-N 2020. CCIS, vol. 1348, pp. 95–119. Springer, Cham (2020). https://doi.org/10.1007/978-3-030-65810-6_6

28. SDN. http://blog.d2-si.fr/2016/01/06/software-defined-network/. Accessed Sept 2021
29. Egidius, P.M., Abu-Mahfouz, A.M., Hancke, G.P.: Programmable node in software-defined wireless sensor networks: a review. In: IECON 2018–44th Annual Conference of the IEEE Industrial Electronics Society, pp. 4672–4677. IEEE (2018)
30. Luo, T., Tan, H.-P., Quek, T.Q.S.: Sensor openflow: enabling software-defined wireless sensor networks. IEEE Commun. Lett. **16**(11), 1896–1899 (2012)
31. De Gante, A., Aslan, M., Matrawy, A.: Smart wireless sensor network management based on software-defined networking. In: 2014 27th Biennial Symposium on Communications (QBSC), pp. 71–75. IEEE (2014)
32. De Oliveira, B.T., Gabriel, L.B., Margi, C.B.: Tinysdn: enabling multiple controllers for software-defined wireless sensor networks. IEEE Latin Am. Trans. **13**(11), 3690–3696 (2015)
33. Costanzo, S., Galluccio, L., Morabito, G., Palazzo, S.: Software defined wireless networks (SDWN): Unbridling SDNs. In: European Workshop on Software Defined Networking, pp. 1–6 (2012)
34. Kobo, H.I., Abu-Mahfouz, A.M., Hancke, G.P.: Challenges and design requirements: a survey on software-defined wireless sensor networks. IEEE Access **5**, 1872–1899 (2017)
35. Ndiaye, M., Hancke, G.P., Abu-Mahfouz, A.M.: Software defined networking for improved wireless sensor network management: a survey. Sensors **17**(5), 1031 (2017)
36. Zhu, Y., Zhang, Y., Xia, W., Shen, L.: A software-defined network based node selection algorithm in WSN localization. In: 2016 IEEE 83rd Vehicular Technology Conference (VTC Spring), pp. 1–5. IEEE (2016)
37. Zhu, Y., Xing, S., Zhang, Y., Yan, F., Shen, L.: Localisation algorithm with node selection under power constraint in software-defined sensor networks. IET Commun. **11**(13), 2035–2041 (2017)
38. Jacobsson, M., Orfanidis, C.: Using software-defined networking principles for wireless sensor networks. In: SNCNW 2015, May 28–29, Karlstad (2015)
39. Jayashree, P., Infant Princy, F.: Leveraging SDN to conserve energy in WSN-an analysis. In: 2015 3rd International Conference on Signal Processing, Communication and Networking (ICSCN), pp. 1–6. IEEE (2015)
40. Wang, Y., Chen, H., Xiaoling, W., Shu, L.: An energy-efficient SDN based sleep scheduling algorithm for WSNs. J. Netw. Comput. Appl. **59**, 39–45 (2016)
41. Tumuluri, R., Kovi, A., Kumar Raju Alluri, B.K.S.P.: An energy-efficient algorithm using layer heads for software-defined wireless sensor networks. In: 2018 International Conference on Recent Trends in Advance Computing (ICRTAC), pp. 103–108. IEEE (2018)
42. Liao, W., Wu, M., Wu, Y.: Energy-efficient algorithm based on multi-dimensional energy space for software-defined wireless sensor networks. In: 2016 International Symposium on Wireless Communication Systems (ISWCS), pp. 309–314. IEEE (2016)
43. Abu-Mahfouz, A.M., Hancke, G.P.: An efficient distributed localisation algorithm for wireless sensor networks: based on smart reference-selection method. Int. J. Sen. Netw. **13**(2), 94–111 (2013)
44. de Oliveira, B.T., Margi, C.B.: Distributed control plane architecture for software-defined wireless sensor networks. In: 2016 IEEE International Symposium on Consumer Electronics (ISCE), pp. 85–86. IEEE (2016)

45. Kobo, H.I., Abu-Mahfouz, A.M., Hancke, G.P.: Fragmentation-based distributed control system for software-defined wireless sensor networks. IEEE Trans. Indust. Inf. **15**(2), 901–910 (2018)

46. Ksouri, C., Jemili, I., Mosbah, M., Belghith, A.: Data gathering for internet of vehicles safety. In: 2018 14th International Wireless Communications & Mobile Computing Conference (IWCMC), pp. 904–909. IEEE (2018)

47. Wikipedia. https://fr.wikipedia.org/wiki/capteur. Accessed Sept 2021

48. Hung, C.-C., Hsieh, C.-C.: Big data management on wireless sensor networks. In: Big Data Analytics for Sensor-Network Collected Intelligence, pp. 99–116. Elsevier (2017)

49. Tao, M., Li, X., Yuan, H., Wei, W.: UAV-aided trustworthy data collection in federated-WSN-enabled IOT applications. Inf. Sci. (2020)

50. Chen, M., Liang, W., Li, Y.: Data collection maximization for UAV-enabled wireless sensor networks. In: 2020 29th International Conference on Computer Communications and Networks (ICCCN), pp. 1–9. IEEE (2020)

51. Yaseen, Q., AlBalas, F., Jararweh, Y., Al-Ayyoub, M.: A fog computing based system for selective forwarding detection in mobile wireless sensor networks. In: 2016 IEEE 1st International Workshops on Foundations and Applications of Self* Systems (FAS* W), pp. 256–262. IEEE (2016)

52. Adhatarao, S.S., Arumaithurai, M., Fu, X.: Fogg: a fog computing based gateway to integrate sensor networks to internet. In: 2017 29th International Teletraffic Congress (ITC 29), vol. 2, pp. 42–47. IEEE (2017)

53. Benomar, Z., Campobello, G., Longo, F., Merlino, G., Puliafito, A.: Fog-enabled industrial WSNs to monitor asynchronous electric motors. In: 2020 IEEE International Conference on Smart Computing (SMARTCOMP), pp. 434–439. IEEE (2020)

54. Mazza, D., Tarchi, D., Corazza, G.E.: A unified urban mobile cloud computing offloading mechanism for smart cities. IEEE Commun. Magaz. **55**(3), 30–37 (2017)

55. Vaquero, L.M., Rodero-Merino, L., Caceres, J., Lindner, M.: A break in the clouds: towards a cloud definition (2008)

56. Petrolo, R., Loscri, V., Mitton, N.: Towards a smart city based on cloud of things. In: Proceedings of the 2014 ACM International Workshop on Wireless and Mobile Technologies for Smart Cities, pp. 61–66. ACM (2014)

57. Comment le Big data impacte le Cloud computing? http://www.zdnet.fr/actualites/comment-le-big-data-impacte-le-cloud-computing-39829534.htm. Accessed Sept 2021

58. Edge to Cloud. https://www.techtarget.com/searchnetworking/answer/fog-computing-vs-edge-computing-whats-the-difference. Accessed Sept 2021

59. Al Nuaimi, E., Al Neyadi, H., Mohamed, N., Al-Jaroodi, J.: Applications of big data to smart cities. J. Internet Serv. Appl. **6**(1), 25 (2015)

60. Ward, J.S., Barker, A.: Undefined by data: a survey of big data definitions. arXiv preprint arXiv:1309.5821 (2013)

61. Rios, L.G. et al.: Big data infrastructure for analyzing data generated by wireless sensor networks. In: 2014 IEEE International Congress on Big Data, pp. 816–823. IEEE (2014)

62. Kim, B.-S., Kim, K.-I., Shah, B., Chow, F., Kim, K.H.: Wireless sensor networks for big data systems. Sensors **19**(7), 1565 (2019)

63. Boubiche, D.E.: Secure and efficient big data gathering in heterogeneous wireless sensor networks. In: Proceedings of the International Conference on Internet of Things and Cloud Computing, p. 1 (2016)

64. Kandah, F.I., Nichols, O., Yang, L.: Efficient key management for big data gathering in dynamic sensor networks. In: 2017 International Conference on Computing, Networking and Communications (ICNC), pp. 667–671. IEEE (2017)
65. Kushalnagar, N., Montenegro, G.: Transmission of IPV6 Packets Over IEEE 802.15. 4 Networks (2007)
66. Grosky, W.I., Kansal, A., Nath, S., Liu, J., Zhao, F.: Senseweb: an infrastructure for shared sensing. IEEE Multim. **14**(4), 8–13 (2007)
67. Durand, J.: Le sdn pour les nuls. Cisco Systems JRES (2015)
68. Shu, Y., et al.: Internet of things: wireless sensor networks. White Paper, International Electrotechnical Commission, http://www.iec.ch, p. 11 (2014)
69. Mukherjee, M., Shu, L., Wang, D.: Survey of fog computing: fundamental, network applications, and research challenges. IEEE Commun. Surv. Tutor. **20**(3), 1826–1857 (2018)
70. Gazis, V., Leonardi, A., Mathioudakis, K., Sasloglou, K., Kikiras, P., Sudhaakar, R.: Components of fog computing in an industrial internet of things context. In: 2015 12th Annual IEEE International Conference on Sensing, Communication, and Networking-Workshops (SECON Workshops), pp. 1–6. IEEE (2015)
71. Mukherjee, M., Shu, L., Wang, D., Li, K., Chen, Y.: A fog computing-based framework to reduce traffic overhead in large-scale industrial applications. In: 2017 IEEE Conference on Computer Communications Workshops (INFOCOM WKSHPS), pp. 1008–1009. IEEE (2017)
72. Das, K., Das, S., Darji, R.K., Mishra, A.: Survey of energy-efficient techniques for the cloud-integrated sensor network. J. Sensors **2018** (2018)
73. Guan, Z., Yang, T., Xiaojiang, D.: Achieving secure and efficient data access control for cloud-integrated body sensor networks. Int. J. Distrib. Sens. Netw. **11**(8), 101287 (2015)
74. Dwivedi, R.K., Saran, M., Kumar, R.: A survey on security over sensor-cloud. In: 2019 9th International Conference on Cloud Computing, Data Science & Engineering (Confluence), pp. 31–37. IEEE (2019)
75. Data. https://sherpasoftware.com/blog/structured-and-unstructured-data-what-is-it/. Accessed Sept 2021

A Survey of Routing Protocols for WSNs in Smart Farming Applications

Karim Fathallah[1]([⊠]) [iD], Mohamed Amine Abid[2] [iD],
and Nejib Ben Hadj-Alouane[1] [iD]

[1] National Engineering School of Tunis, University of Tunis El Manar, Tunis, Tunisia
fathallah.karim@gmail.com
[2] National School of Computer Science, University of Manouba, Manouba, Tunisia

Abstract. Wireless sensor networks (WSNs) are used in various applications ranging from military to home automation and smart farming. WSNs are deployed to sense the environment so that decision-management systems can make appropriate monitoring and thoughtful decisions. In most cases, sensory data is routed from sensor nodes towards a sink node, used as a gateway towards tiers where the data is used (e.g., preprocessing, backup in a database, decision-making). In this paper, we propose to survey the state-of-the-art of routing protocols for sensor networks in the field of smart farming.

Keywords: Smart Farming · Internet of Things · Wireless Sensor Network · Routing Protocols

1 Introduction

A wireless sensor network is composed of nodes capable of actuating/sensing the environment, processing the sensed data, and communicating it to other nodes. Once deployed, the nodes cooperate autonomously to transmit the data to a base station through which monitoring and/or control activities can be performed. Nowadays, using WSNs in farming became mandatory and with a very high and tangible added value.

Smart farming applications are used in order to optimize crop production and resource usage. They cover a wide range of monitored types of crops in diversified facilities: vineyards [5], greenhouses monitoring [38], horticulture [18], soil moisture monitoring in irrigation applications [41] or pest prevention [37].

The monitored field can correspond to a large area (farmland) requiring many sensors spread all over the field or a specific building like a greenhouse with relatively small but dense WSNs. It is mandatory to rely on a routing protocol that suits the considered smart farming application in both cases. The routing protocol is required to enable data exchange between the deployed sensor nodes and a decision management system usually hosted in the cloud and accessible via a gateway or a sink node.

I. Jemili and M. Mosbah (Eds.): DiCES-N 2022, CCIS 1564, pp. 24–37, 2022.
https://doi.org/10.1007/978-3-030-99004-6_2

In this paper, Sect. 2 presents the smart farming background and identifies the requirements for routing protocols in WSNs in the context of smart farming. Section 3 surveys the literature of the most used routing protocols in smart farming applications. In Sect. 4, we compare the list of surveyed protocols in terms of the identified smart farming requirements. Finally, Sect. 5 concludes the paper.

2 Background

2.1 Smart Farming

Smart Agriculture, or Smart Farming, refers to the management of farms using modern information and communication technologies. It aims at increasing the quantity and quality of products while optimizing the required resources and human labor. In modern smart farms, technologies like drones, robots, farm machinery, wireless sensor/actuator networks, decision support systems in the cloud, etc., are deployed. Armed with these tools, farmers can monitor field conditions from anywhere and anytime and make strategic decisions for the entire farm or targeted partitions of the farm, allowing a sustainable intensification of the production and optimization of used resources. Such applications rely on a communication backbone offered by a deployed wireless sensor network (WSN), where different smart objects and devices are interconnected to exchange sensed data or to command specific actuation. This backbone is of most importance, as it enables the automation of processes, control, and decision-making.

In smart farms, this communication backbone is usually composed of wireless sensor networks, with the task of sensing and/or actuating on the environment; a sink node alternatively called a base station, in which sensed data is wirelessly transmitted via the deployed sensor nodes; and a monitoring and decision-making application hosted in the cloud where the sensed data received from the sink is processed and consequent decisions are generated. These decisions, translated into actuation commands or configuration commands, are sent back through the reverse path towards the sensor and actuator nodes to be executed. The goal is to provide assistance to the farmer and perform agricultural tasks such as irrigation, use of pesticides, etc. Of course, the type of sensors and actuators to use depends on the deployed application: what type of data do we need to sense (e.g., temperature, humidity, moisture), or what type of actuation are we optimizing (e.g., irrigation, fertilization, pest control). It can also be decided by the need for static nodes or nodes supporting mobility.

Nevertheless, and independent of the type of deployed sensors, the WSN is required to perform well in conveying data and commands back and forth and as long as deployed. In fact, the automation processes offered by any smart farming application can only achieve their goals if data and commands are received correctly and timely. Besides, the main advantages of using wireless sensors are the flexibility of deployment, the ease of maintenance, and the little required human intervention in the field. In other terms, a deployed WSN has to achieve its communication task by defining a communication procedure between its nodes that satisfies the application constraints and requirements. At the same time, it preserves its lifetime and overcomes faults that might occur. This procedure is called the routing protocol, responsible for routing exchanged data/commands from a source node towards a specific destination. It defines how the WSN is logically structured, the needed information to be exchanged to maintain this structure, and eventually healing procedures to recover from potential failures. The routing protocol shall be designed in a way that respects the application's needs and requirements.

2.2 Requirements for WSN Routing in the Smart Farming Context

Routing in WSNs is widely addressed in the literature [3,39]. However, the suitability of a routing protocol depends closely on the application where it is used. In fact, the farming context, for instance, differs deeply from other applications like smart grids or smart homes. Consequently, despite the tremendous number of routing protocols for WSNs found in the literature, only a few are practically used in a realistic context. An even smaller fraction is deployed in smart farming applications. Generally, for a routing protocol in a WSN to suit a smart farming application, it has to fulfill the following list of application requirements:

Energy Efficiency: A WSN deployed in farmland must remain active during successive crop cycles. This takes months or even years. During this time, the WSN nodes need to remain up and running, extending the network lifetime as long as possible. Knowing that 75% of the nodes' energy is used for the transmission of packets [30], the used routing protocol, the orchestrator of all communications in the network, plays a key role in energy conservation and efficiency (e.g., reducing the number of transmissions performed to route the data, using load-balancing techniques, using adaptive communication rates). For example, it is intuitive to see that clustered and hierarchical routing protocols have more potential to achieve energy conservation compared to flat routing protocols.

Robustness: Robustness, or more generally Fault-Tolerance, shall be a requirement for a routing protocol in the smart farming context. Wireless sensor nodes rely on batteries to run. Whatever energy conservation is applied, these batteries will be depleted at some point in time, and the sensor node will die. In an agricultural application, the larger the number of dead nodes, the less effective and more unstable the WSN would be. A robust routing protocol is a protocol that manages to sustain its needed functionality despite the loss of some nodes and thus communication links. The robustness of a routing protocol can be measured as the number of failing links and nodes that the routing protocol can withstand by assuring stable functioning.

Scalability: Depending on the smart farming application, a WSN can have more or less high node density. Generally, for large open space agriculture applications, the monitored agricultural fields, pasture lands, and sites measure tens or hundreds of acres in area, so the number of deployed sensor nodes can vary from dozens to thousands. The ability to handle a large number of sensor nodes and ensure full coverage of the monitored area defines the scalability of the routing protocol [34]. Besides, the initial WSN setup is usually never kept the same over time: typically, new nodes are added during the lifetime of the network, while others are lost as they may die. The newly added nodes should be dynamically included and handled without requiring a full network reset. The way the routing protocol logically structures the network impacts how easy/hard hosting new nodes is. This defines another important aspect of the scalability of the routing protocol. For example, hierarchical networks, electing special nodes, called clusters, distributed throughout the network, are expected to be more scalable than flat routing protocols.

Interoperability: Generally, a smart farming application requires the deployment of a heterogeneous WSN. In fact, an integrated smart farm is composed of multiple specialized parcels and buildings. In each part, equipment of different kinds are deployed: sensors, robots, drones, special machinery, etc. All these equipment are interconnected and forming a WSN. The ability of the routing algorithm to efficiently support all these equipment independently of the nodes' technologies is called *interoperability* [21].

Querying: For optimization purposes, many smart farming applications abstract a WSN and virtually represent it as a distributed database. This approach is called the *sensor database approach* [19]. The WSN is viewed as a relational database, queried using SQL-like languages as a means for query description and processing. It offers smart farming applications a comprehensive and easy-to-use querying system to be used to reliably and accurately retrieve information about the monitored field on-demand and with minimal delay. The ability of the routing protocol to support such querying systems and optimally integrate them (e.g., by allowing spatial queries or In-Network Aggregation) represents a big plus in the smart farming context.

3 Routing Protocols for WSNs in Agriculture Applications

A routing protocol in wireless sensor networks describes how to route a message from a sending node to a specified destination. The decision on which path to follow can be based on several metrics such as the number of hops, geographic location, end-to-end delay, etc. Generally, WSN routing protocols can be classified either according to how they establish routing paths or the way they logically structure the network [4].

Routing protocols can build routing routes either proactively or re-actively [4]. Proactive protocols calculate all routes from each node towards all others in the network before they are actually needed (i.e., proactively) and store them in routing tables in each node. Route changes must be propagated throughout the network to maintain a consistent distributed knowledge of the network topology among all nodes (to avoid loop formation and outdated entries). This implies a significant overhead for building and maintaining routing tables at each node. Reactive protocols, on the other hand, only calculate routes when needed. Before transmitting a stream of data, an exploration process is initiated to locate the destination node in the network and build a routing path towards it. Healing/recovery mechanisms are used to recover from link breakages on established paths. While reactive protocols induce less routing overhead than proactive protocols, they require more time to route the data to the ultimate destination. Finally, hybrid protocols combine the mechanisms used by both proactive and reactive protocols.

Routing protocols in WSNs can also be categorized based on the type of network logical structure they build as flat or hierarchical [4]. Flat protocols treat all nodes in the network as having the same capabilities and thus, all nodes participate equally in the routing tasks. This implies that the closer we get to the sink, the higher is the participation of nodes because most of the traffic is routed towards the sink through its direct neighbors. Adversely, in hierarchical protocols, the network is logically structured in clusters of nodes. For each cluster, a special node, called the cluster head, is elected. Rather than routing data from the nodes directly to the sink through individual paths, nodes in a cluster send messages only to the cluster leader. The cluster head has the responsibility to transmit all cluster messages to the designated receiver. This allows mechanisms such as aggregation to be implemented.

Many research works on the development, analysis, and adoption of routing protocols for WSNs in the agricultural context can be found in the literature. In this section, we present the most widely used routing protocols for agricultural applications.

3.1 ZigBee-AODV (ZigBee Ad-hoc On-Demand Distance Vector) Routing Protocol

Due to the massive adoption of the ZigBee [6] technology by the wireless sensor network community and its integration in largely adopted wireless sensor nodes, the ZigBee is utilized in numerous WSN deployments in the smart farming context. In [20], authors present an application for control and monitoring in smart irrigation systems. In [36] authors describe a generic low-power and low-cost field data acquisition system that supports remote control over ZigBee networks for farm management operations. In [33], the authors designed an intelligent greenhouse environment monitoring system based on ZigBee technology. In [44] authors introduce a low-cost wireless sensor node supporting ZigBee, used for orchard monitoring.

ZigBee [6] uses mesh routing to establish a route between a source node and a destination node. Mesh routing allows data packets to transit through multiple nodes in a network to get from a source to a destination. Intermediate nodes participate in establishing the route between the source and the destination reactively, using a process called route discovery. In the ZigBee-AODV [32], the route discovery process is based on the AODV protocol [12].

The route discovery is a broadcast process (illustrated in Fig. 1) triggered by a node and forwarded by all nodes hearing the route request command if they cannot answer it (i.e., no routes towards the sought destination are known). A route request command embeds the cost of the routes in terms of the number of hops (i.e., the field is incremented by every node forwarding the request). The destination accumulates the route requests received from its neighbors and issues a route reply packet through the reverse path with the least cost (Fig. 2). Routing decisions (i.e., the next hop to reach on the route towards a given destination) are cached at intermediate nodes to be used during the communication session. If the next hop is not known, route discovery is triggered to find/recover a path. Since the cash memory size is usually limited, only a small number of routes can be stored simultaneously. As such, the route discovery process is triggered more often on a large network with communication between many different nodes.

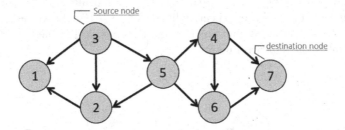

Fig. 1. Route discovery process: route request

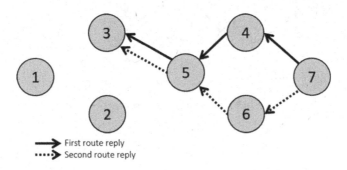

Fig. 2. Route discovery process: route reply

3.2   XMesh Routing Protocol

XMesh [35] is a multi-hop routing protocol developed by Crossbow Inc. [27] to run on the MICA and EKO Pro family of motes [15]. EKO Pro family represents the first farming specialized wireless sensor network solution of Crossbow Inc. This technology was largely adopted before the generalization of the ZigBee-based WSNs.

To build routing paths, XMesh uses a cost metric, called the Minimum Transmission (MT), representing the minimal total number of transmissions in delivering a packet over multiple hops to a given destination. This metric turns to be extremely useful when the transmission links in the network are of varying quality (which is the case in many agricultural applications). In fact, routing through a longer path with fewer retransmissions is better in terms of overall energy consumption than using a shorter unreliable path with many retransmissions.

Periodically, all nodes in the network broadcast beacon messages. A beacon message contains an estimate of the MT, indicating to the node's neighbors, the total energy required to transmit a message from the node itself towards the sink. The beacon also contains a list of the node's neighboring motes (NL) with an estimate of the quality of the respective links. A node receiving a beacon message compiles the information it contains to update its own MT value (Fig. 3), before sharing it in the next beacon period.

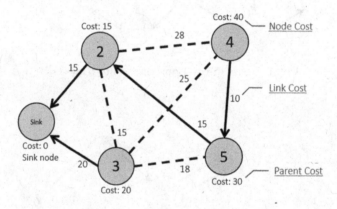

Fig. 3. Xmesh routing protocol

3.3   Low Energy Adaptive Clustering Hierarchy (LEACH)

Low Energy Adaptive Clustering Hierarchy (LEACH) [22] is considered as the first hierarchical routing protocol for WSNs. Although it was first proposed in early 2000, LEACH recently gained interest, especially in agriculture applications. Actually, there are plenty of variant LEACH-based protocols optimized for different fields of application. A recent study in [11] has shown higher reliability of LEACH in large area farming deployments when compared to other protocols like AODV. [40] and [7] proposed new, improved variants of LEACH adapted for precision agriculture applications and showed a significant improvement in terms of energy consumption compared to other used protocols. LEACH's good performance in terms of energy conservation is also demonstrated in [25] where the authors give a detailed performance evaluation of the protocol used in an agriculture application.

The WSN operation runs through two successive steps called setup phase and steady-state. During the setup, LEACH structures the network into clusters of nodes (see Fig. 4). The cluster formation is performed periodically by randomly selecting a small number of cluster heads (CHs). Each CH notifies its own role to its direct neighbors using a broadcast message. The other nodes, alerted by this message, decide which cluster to join based on the signal strength and inform the corresponding CH about their membership. The clustering is repeated periodically to make sure that the CH role is rotated evenly between the nodes.

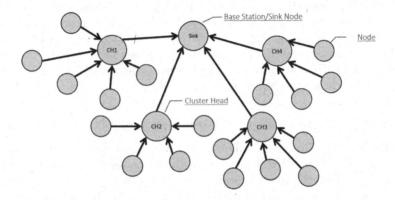

Fig. 4. LEACH

In the second phase, the data transfer inside the cluster and to the base station (BS)/sink node occurs. The CH collects data coming from the nodes in the cluster, aggregates them, and compresses them before sending them to the BS. To reduce the possible collisions inside the cluster or between different clusters, the CH node establishes a TDMA schedule and assigns a time slot to each node in the cluster. This schedule is shared with the cluster members via a broadcast message and used by the cluster members until a new setup phase is launched. The data collection can be made either periodically or asynchronously, making it suitable for constant monitoring activities.

3.4   Threshold Sensitive Energy Efficient Sensor Network Protocol

The Threshold Sensitive Energy Efficient Sensor Network protocol (TEEN) [28] and the Adaptive Threshold Sensitive Energy Efficient Sensor Network protocol (APTEEN) [29] are hierarchical, reactive routing protocols. Many research studies and applications investigated using TEEN and APTEEN in the context of smart farming. In [1] authors used APTEEN in a potato pest prevention application. In [10] authors proposed an optimized variant of APTEEN in an application monitoring and controlling the cultivation of sugarcane crops. In [2], authors have shown a higher energy efficiency of TEEN compared to LEACH-based routing algorithms in a smart farming context. [31] conducted a performance comparison between LEACH, TEEN, and APTEEN in a smart farming context and showed higher energy conservation for APTEEN.

TEEN structures the network in a very similar way to LEACH. Clusters are formed, a TDMA schedule is calculated, and shared cluster members send data to the cluster head, and the cluster head is responsible for reaching the BS. Unlike LEACH, TEEN defines two thresholds: the hard threshold(HT) and the soft threshold (ST). They are used to control the quantity of data transmission by only allowing nodes to report data of interest, i.e., within a range of interest to the user, and/or have changed significantly since the last reporting time. With the TDMA schedule, the cluster head broadcasts the values of HT and ST to be used. A sensor node sends a data message only if the current sensed value is greater than TH and differs from the previously reported value by at least ST. The cluster head also specifies the reporting frequency to be used by the cluster members. APTEEN is a variant of TEEN where cluster heads are additionally responsible for data aggregation and energy saving.

3.5   Routing Protocol for Low-Power and Lossy Networks

RPL [43] (Routing Protocol for Low-Power and Lossy Networks) is a routing protocol conceived for wireless networks with low power consumption and lossy transmission. Recently, many research contributions considered applying the RPL protocol in the context of smart farming. In [26], the authors proposed a data aggregation scheme for low-power and lossy networks based on RPL. RPL conveys collected sensory data from the monitored agricultural field, e.g., a greenhouse, towards the monitoring application. [13] proposes an adaptation of RPL used for the monitoring of a smart farm. This adaptation combines the awareness of energy, reliability, and robustness in a composite routing metric used to derive the routing paths. In [8], the authors proposed an approach to tune some RPL parameters to minimize energy consumption while assuring an acceptable performance level. In [30], the authors explored how to apply RPL for smart irrigation systems. [16] describes an RPL-based protocol that builds a routing topology taking into account the spatial partition of the monitored farmland. The proposed protocol demonstrated improvement in energy consumption when applied in realistic smart farming scenarios [14]. Moreover, higher performance was achieved when in-network spatial query processing is applied [17].

RPL is a distance-vector protocol. As shown in Fig. 5, RPL structures the network as a destination-oriented directed acyclic graph (DODAG). It is a tree-like topology rooted at the sink node and contains the paths from the root to the leaves. The DODAG is built by exchanging DIO messages. In RPL, the upward routing traffic is based on the DODAG. To reach the sink node, every node addresses its message to its preferred parent (as indicated by the DODAG).

The preferred parent does the same until the sink node is reached. For the downstream traffic, RPL uses DAO messages to maintain routing tables. RPL is considered to have a hierarchical topology.

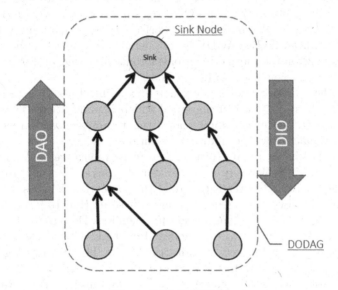

Fig. 5. RPL DODAG

4   Discussion

After presenting some of the most used routing protocols in WSNs in the context of smart farming, we devote the present section to compare them in terms of the smart farming requirements identified in Sect. 2.2. Table 1 summaries our findings.

Table 1. Suitability of the selected routing protocols to the smart farming requirements

Algorithm	Energy efficiency	Scalability	Interoperability	Robustness	Querying
ZIGBEE-AODV	+	−	−	++	−−
XMESH	+	−	−	++	−−
LEACH-based	++	++	−	+	−
TEEN/APTEEN	++	++	−	+	+/−
RPL-based	+++	+++	++	++	+

The ZigBee mesh routing is similar to AODV as it requires triggering a flooding mechanism (i.e., route discovery) whenever new traffic needs to be routed.

While this might help reduce energy consumption, it causes scalability issues as the number of nodes in the network and/or data traffic streams increases and induces significant end-to-end delays. Besides, as this protocol only supports the ZigBee technology, it obviously presents interoperability limitations. Moreover, being a reactive protocol, ZigBee-AODV does not impose any logical topology structure, making it very hard and tedious to integrate querying systems. In terms of robustness, ZigBee-AODV is considered robust as the impact of dying nodes is very low on the routing functions: a route discovery process is triggered whenever a destination needs to be reached.

In [42], the XMesh protocol is evaluated experimentally. It is proven to be reliable and robust. However, it presented scalability limitations. Despite being designed to serve agriculture applications, this technology was rarely deployed and quickly replaced by other industrial solutions.

On the other hand, LEACH was proven to be robust, reliable, and energy-efficient. Besides, it scales very well thanks to its hierarchical nature. In terms of induced delays, LEACH tends to reduce the contention delay as it relies on a TDMA schedule; however, it requires a periodic setup time to form clusters, fix the schedule, and share it among the cluster members. Despite the high number of research works interested in the applicability of LEACH in real applications, the protocol is not used largely in industrial WSNs. Its built topology changes drastically from one period to the next one, making it very hard and complex to integrate additional services such as querying and in-network aggregation.

Similar to LEACH, TEEN/APTEEN represent good candidates for smart farming applications. [29] presents an attempt to implement more advanced energy-saving mechanisms as well as in-network data aggregation mechanisms. However, such additional mechanisms remain hard to be integrated as, like LEACH, the built topology is constantly and drastically changing over time. TEEN/APTEEN are not largely deployed in industrial WSNs.

Finally, RPL-based routing protocols are based on IPv6, which ensures very high interoperability. RPL is also hierarchical, making it scalable and energy-efficient. Besides, many studies [23] prove the robustness of RPL and its suitability to time-sensitive applications. Moreover, many RPL-based proposals detail how querying and spatial querying [17], in-network aggregation [9], or multicast [24] services can be easily integrated and supported.

5   Conclusion

In this paper, we surveyed the routing protocols for WSNs in the context of smart farming. The protocols were presented and then compared in terms of identified requirements for smart farming applications. Our study showed that the suitability of the routing protocol depends on the targeted application. It also shows that most proposed protocols address energy conservation and rely on more or less sophisticated energy-preserving mechanisms. Besides, scalability, robustness, and interoperability in a farming application remain important criteria for a routing protocol to be practically used.

References

1. Abd El-kader, S.M., Mohammad El-Basioni, B.M.: Precision farming solution in Egypt using the wireless sensor network technology. Egypt. Inf. J. **14**(3), 221–233 (2013)
2. Abedin, Z., Paul, S., Akhter, S., Siddiquee, K.N.A., Hossain, M.S., Andersson, K.: Selection of energy efficient routing protocol for irrigation enabled by wireless sensor network. In: 2017 IEEE 42nd Conference on Local Computer Networks Workshops (LCN Workshops), pp. 75–81. IEEE (2017)
3. Akkaya, K., Younis, M.: A survey on routing protocols for wireless sensor networks. Ad Hoc Netw. **3**(3), 325–349 (2005)
4. Al-Karaki, J.N., Kamal, A.E.: Routing techniques in wireless sensor networks: a survey. IEEE Wirel. Commun. **11**(6), 6–28 (2004)
5. Alippi, C., Boracchi, G., Camplani, R., Roveri, M.: Wireless sensor networks for monitoring vineyards. In: Anastasi, G., Bellini, E., Di Nitto, E., Ghezzi, C., Tanca, L., Zimeo, E. (eds.) Methodologies and Technologies for Networked Enterprises. LNCS, vol. 7200, pp. 295–310. Springer, Heidelberg (2012). https://doi.org/10.1007/978-3-642-31739-2_15
6. Alliance, Z.: Zigbee alliance. WPAN industry group (2010). The industry group responsible for the ZigBee standard and certification. http://www.zigbee.org/
7. Anand, S.J., et al.: IoT-based secure and energy efficient scheme for precision agriculture using blockchain and improved LEACH algorithm. Turk. J. Comput. Math. Educ. (TURCOMAT) **12**(10), 2466–2475 (2021)
8. ArunKumar, M., Alagumeenaakshi, M.: RPL optimization for precise green house management using wireless sensor network. In: 2014 International Conference on Green Computing Communication and Electrical Engineering (ICGCCEE), pp. 1–6. IEEE (2014)
9. Bahramlou, A., Javidan, R.: Adaptive timing model for improving routing and data aggregation in internet of things networks using RPL. IET Netw. **7**(5), 306–312 (2018)
10. Bhagyashree, S., Prashanthi, S., Anandkumar, K.: Enhancing network lifetime in precision agriculture using APTEEN protocol. In: 2015 IEEE Technological Innovation in ICT for Agriculture and Rural Development (TIAR), pp. 44–48. IEEE (2015)
11. Cagnetti, M., Leccisi, M., Leccese, F.: Reliability comparison of routing protocols for WSNs in wide agriculture scenarios by means of ηl index. In: Proceedings of the 9th International Conference on Sensor Networks, SENSORNETS 2020, pp. 169–176 (2020)
12. Chakeres, I.D., Belding-Royer, E.M.: AODV routing protocol implementation design. In: 2004 Proceedings of the 24th International Conference on Distributed Computing Systems Workshops, pp. 698–703. IEEE (2004)
13. Chen, Y., Chanet, J.P., Hou, K.M., Shi, H., De Sousa, G.: A scalable context-aware objective function (SCAOF) of routing protocol for agricultural low-power and lossy networks (RPAL). Sensors **15**(8), 19507–19540 (2015)
14. Fathallah, K., Abid, M.A., Ben Hadj-Alouane, N.: Enhancing energy saving in smart farming through aggregation and partition aware IoT routing protocol. Sensors **20**(10), 2760 (2020)
15. Fathallah, K., Abid, M.A., Hadj-Alouane, N.B.: Internet of things in the service of precision agriculture (2017)

16. Fathallah, K., Abid, M.A., Hadj-Alouane, N.B.: PA-RPL: a partition aware IoT routing protocol for precision agriculture. In: 2018 14th International Wireless Communications & Mobile Computing Conference (IWCMC), pp. 672–677. IEEE (2018)

17. Fathallah, K., Abid, M.A., Hadj-Alouane, N.B.: Routing of spatial queries over IoT enabled wireless sensor networks. In: 2019 15th International Wireless Communications & Mobile Computing Conference (IWCMC), pp. 1779–1784. IEEE (2019)

18. Ghutke, P.C., Agrawal, R.: The usage of IoT and far off sensor associations and their application in horticulture for the improvement of yield efficiency in India (2021)

19. Govindan, R., Hellerstein, J., Hong, W., Madden, S., Franklin, M., Shenker, S.: The sensor network as a database. Technical report. Citeseer (2002)

20. Goyal, S.P., Bhise, A.: ZigBee based real-time monitoring system of agricultural environment. Int. J. Eng. Res. Appl. $4(2)$, 06–09 (2014)

21. Halder, S., Bit, S.D.: Enhancement of wireless sensor network lifetime by deploying heterogeneous nodes. J. Netw. Comput. Appl. 38, 106–124 (2014)

22. Heinzelman, W.R., Chandrakasan, A., Balakrishnan, H.: Energy-efficient communication protocol for wireless microsensor networks. In: Proceedings of the 33rd Annual Hawaii International Conference on System Sciences, p. 10. IEEE (2000)

23. Heurtefeux, K., Menouar, H., AbuAli, N.: Experimental evaluation of a routing protocol for WSNs: RPL robustness under study. In: 2013 IEEE 9th International Conference on Wireless and Mobile Computing, Networking and Communications (WiMob), pp. 491–498. IEEE (2013)

24. Hwang, R.H., Peng, M.C., Wu, C.Y., Abimannan, S.: A novel RPL-based multicast routing mechanism for wireless sensor networks. Int. J. Ad Hoc Ubiquit. Comput. $33(2)$, 122–131 (2020)

25. Kamarudin, L.M., Ahmad, R.B., Ndzi, D.L., Zakaria, A., Kamarudin, K., Ahmed, M.E.E.S.: Simulation and analysis of leach for wireless sensor networks in agriculture. Int. J. Sensor Netw. $21(1)$, 16–26 (2016)

26. Kim, Y., Bae, P., Han, J., Ko, Y.B.: Data aggregation in precision agriculture for low-power and lossy networks. In: 2015 IEEE Pacific Rim Conference on Communications, Computers and Signal Processing (PACRIM), pp. 438–443. IEEE (2015)

27. Kundargi, K., Sharma, V.: The crossbow^{TM} technology

28. Manjeshwar, A., Agrawal, D.P.: TEEN: a routing protocol for enhanced efficiency in wireless sensor networks. In: IPDPS. vol. 1, p. 189 (2001)

29. Manjeshwar, A., Agrawal, D.P.: APTEEN: a hybrid protocol for efficient routing and comprehensive information retrieval in wireless sensor networks. In: International Parallel and Distributed Processing Symposium, vol. 3, p. 0195b. Citeseer (2002)

30. Öberg, K., Simonsson, J.: System design choices in smart autonomous networked irrigation systems (2014)

31. Parmar, J., Pirishothm, A.: Study of wireless sensor networks using LEACH, TEEN and APTEEN routing protocols. Int. J. Sci. Res. (IJSR) 5, 1221–1224 (2015). ISSN 2319-7064

32. Piyare, R., Lee, S.: Performance analysis of XBee ZB module based wireless sensor networks. Int. J. Sci. Eng. Res. $4(4)$, 1615–1621 (2013)

33. Qiu, W., Dong, L., Wang, F., Yan, H.: Design of intelligent greenhouse environment monitoring system based on ZigBee and embedded technology. In: 2014 IEEE International Conference on Consumer Electronics, China, pp. 1–3. IEEE (2014)

34. Rajput, A., Kumaravelu, V.B.: Scalable and sustainable wireless sensor networks for agricultural application of internet of things using fuzzy c-means algorithm. Sustain. Comput. Inf. Syst. **22**, 62–74 (2019)
35. Sakthipriya, N.: An effective method for crop monitoring using wireless sensor network. Middle-East J. Sci. Res. **20**(9), 1127–1132 (2014)
36. Seyhan, T.G., Kahya, Y., Çamurcu, S., et al.: Feasibility study on using ZigBee networks in agricultural applications. In: Proceedings of the VII International Scientific Agriculture Symposium, Agrosym 2016, Jahorina, Bosnia and Herzegovina, 6–9 October 2016, pp. 2264–2270. Faculty of Agriculture, University of East Sarajevo (2016)
37. Sharma, R.P., Ramesh, D., Pal, P., Tripathi, S., Kumar, C.: IoT-enabled IEEE 802.15.4 WSN monitoring infrastructure-driven fuzzy-logic-based crop pest prediction. IEEE IoT J. **9**(4), 3037–3045 (2022)
38. Shinde, D., Siddiqui, N.: IoT based environment change monitoring & controlling in greenhouse using WSN. In: 2018 International Conference on Information, Communication, Engineering and Technology (ICICET), pp. 1–5. IEEE (2018)
39. Singh, S.K., Singh, M., Singh, D.K., et al.: Routing protocols in wireless sensor networks - a survey. Int. J. Comput. Sci. Eng. Surv. (IJCSES) **1**(2), 63–83 (2010)
40. Soni, K., Hussain, R.: Energy conservation through leach cluster head algorithm in WSN based precision agriculture. Int. J. Sci. Eng. Res. **6**, 166–171 (2015)
41. Srinidhi, J.A., Aasish, A., Kumar, N.K., Ramakrishnaiah, T.: WSN smart irrigation system and weather report system. IOP Conf. Ser. Mater. Sci. Eng. **1042**(1), 012018 (2021)
42. Teo, A., Singh, G., McEachen, J.C.: Evaluation of the XMesh routing protocol in wireless sensor networks. In: 2006 49th IEEE International Midwest Symposium on Circuits and Systems, vol. 2, pp. 113–117. IEEE (2006)
43. Winter, T., et al.: RPL: IPv6 routing protocol for low-power and lossy networks, RFC 6550, pp. 1–157 (2012)
44. Xie, N.: Design of orchard monitoring node based on ZigBee technology (2020)

Leveraging Machine Learning for WBANs

Rim Negra[✉][iD]

ENSI, University of Manouba, Manouba, Tunisia
rim.negra@gmail.com

Abstract. Wireless Body Area Networks are considered as an effective solution for a wide range of healthcare, military and sports applications. These applications are responsible for gathering and managing a huge amount of heterogeneous data from the human body or the surrounding environment in both real and non-real time manners. Relevant information for various fields can be extracted from the raw data. Recently, Machine learning has been extensively explored for real-time big data processing. Thus, the machine learning techniques are very useful for the big data analytic process. In this paper, we discuss the importance of the machine learning techniques use in the fusion and the treatment of the WBAN data, useful for different fields of applications.

Keywords: Wireless Body Area Networks · Machine learning · Prediction · Big data

1 Introduction

In the past few years, the continuous biofeedback monitoring has promoted the development of new technologies related to miniaturized sensors and physiological signal acquisition systems for the information extraction with the minimum discomfort. In this context, Wireless body area networks (WBANs), which are nowadays wide spreading in many academic and industrial fields, are promising effective solutions in ambulatory monitoring, ambient assisted living and pervasive computing systems as well as in sport, gaming, security, entertainment and military fields [1,2]. Besides, the wide spread use of tablets, smartphones and smartwatches as well as the integration of sensors in mobile devices propel the proliferation of mobile health, designed for patients and even for healthy persons. When combined with WBANs, mobile applications can provide important contributions to AAL[1] solutions. These gadgets and systems, collecting sensed data from patients, elder people or individuals in real time, are generating a huge amount of data. Generally, a medical dataset contains thousand of millions of patient data for different diseases or individual status. This massive volume of data could not be handled by traditional tools and techniques for data processing [3]. That's why several algorithms are developed in order to process such huge amount of data. In medical context, applying these techniques with different

---

[1] AAL: Ambient Assisted Living.

I. Jemili and M. Mosbah (Eds.): DiCES-N 2022, CCIS 1564, pp. 38–59, 2022.
https://doi.org/10.1007/978-3-030-99004-6_3

combinations of data collected from different sources can be used to provide a meaningful patient state interpretations [4]. Thus, a smart medical system may be defined as the combination of several data input collected from various body sensors combined with machine learning techniques is able to provide more effective and adaptive solutions. Furthermore, these kinds of systems are expected to promote innovations in the medical area.

In this context, we get recourse to machine learning to deal with this large amount of datasets for processing and data analysis. Machine learning is the subset of artificial intelligence, used for various purposes such as classification, regression and clustering [5]. Machine learning is defined as the automatic detection of relevant patterns in large and complex datasets [6]. In machine learning, systems are trained to behave accordingly. A system can adapt its activities and react to specific situations when it is fed a large volume of data. Several work dealing with WBANs applications got recourse to machine learning techniques in their researches.

Our main objective is to investigate the importance of the use of machine learning in WBAN context. In [7], authors made review for some studies using machine learning for healthcare. In [8], authors explained how to use machine learning techniques for wearable IoT-based applications and outlined the key design factors required to apply such techniques. In [9], introduced the concepts of machine learning and the associated algorithms and presented some case studies. Our comprehensive survey tackles Machine Learning use in WBANs while focusing on the utility of such modeling techniques for a better processing and data interpretation.

The present paper is structured as follows. In Sect. 2, we briefly introduce WBANs. In Sect. 3, we explain the three categories of the machine learning. In Sect. 4, we detail the use of different kinds of machine learning in WBAN applications. In Sect. 5, we discuss the current state and we expose some future open challenges. Finally, we conclude the paper.

2 Overview of Wireless Body Area Networks

As illustrated in Fig. 1, a basic WBAN consists on a set of sensors attached on the human body or implanted under the skin in order to gather specific vital signs such as heart rate, blood pressure, oxygen saturation, etc. Data is collected by the coordinator node; this data is either treated locally or forwarded via the internet to the hosted applications on the cloud computing for further analysis and interpretation [10]. These body sensors are able to communicate with mobile devices such as PDA[2] or smartphones via short-range communications, like Zigbee [11] or Bluetooth [12], as summarized in Table 1.

WBANs offer many innovative applications. In [1], the authors present the main applications of WBANs and highlight their quality of service requirements, mainly:

---

[2] PDA: Personal Digital Assistant.

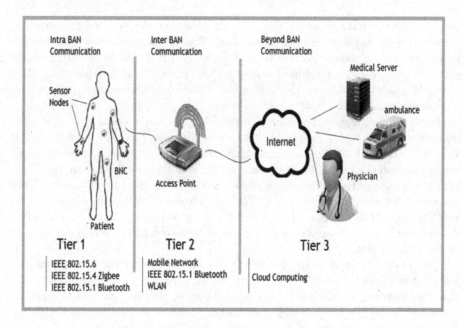

Fig. 1. WBAN Architecture

- Telemedicine and remote patient monitoring to serve and monitor more patients and individuals remotely.
- Rehabilitation and therapy to allow patients to regain their normal functional abilities, through suitable rehabilitation treatments after surgery, by detecting and tracking human movements to rectify any undesired movement[13], as illustrated in Fig. 2.a.
- Biofeedback to enable self-monitoring of the human body.
- Ambient Assisted Living to remotely manage people with disabilities and the elderly who are not regarded as independent but do not require 24-hour medical care [14], as shown in Fig. 2.b.

WBANs have to face many challenges:

- Limited Resources: WBANs are composed of tiny bio-sensors, having limited power, computational capabilities and memory. Generally, these sensors are able to perform easy basic tasks to decrease the energy consumption and prolong the battery lifetime. In fact, these devices have work for many months without changing the battery in many applications.
- Wireless channel: The human body represents a medium with numerous wireless transmission issues; the signal level and propagation from an implanted sensor to a remote destination are unpredictable. Besides, the channel variation is affected mainly by the change in body posture since the body movement may modify the distance between sensors and causes channel variability.

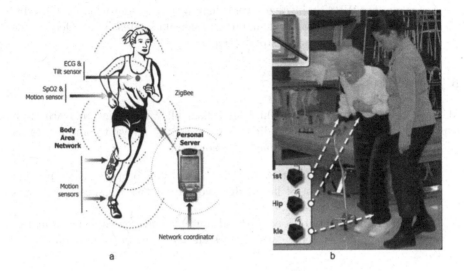

Fig. 2. Examples of WBAN Applications [13,14]

Table 1. Wireless Technologies for WBANs

Technology/ Metrics	IEEE 802.15.1 Bluetooth	IEEE 802.15.4 (ZigBee)	IEEE 802.15.6
Physical Layer	NB[a]	NB	NB, UWB[b], HBC[c]
Range	10 m, 30 m, 100 m	10–30 m	0.1–5 m
Power Consumption	100 mW	60–70 mW	0.1–40 mW
latency	100 ms	Low	Medical applications: 125 ms Non-medical applications: 250 ms
Topology	Master/Slave Piconet	Star Mesh	Star
Frequency	2.4 GHz	2.4 GHz 915 MHz 868 MHz	2.4, 3.1–10.6 GHz 13.5, 50, 400, 600, 900 MHz 402–405 MHz
Data Rate	1 Mbps	250K/40K/20 Kb/s	up to 10 Mbps
Channel Access	TDD[d] TDMA[f]	CSMA/CA[e] TDMA	CSMA/CA, Slotted Aloha TDMA polling
Network size	8	65535	64
Data Transmission Medium	Air	Air	Air, On-Body In-Body

[a] NB: NarrowBand
[b] UWB: Ultra-Wide Band
[c] HBC: Human Body Communications
[d] TDD: Time Division Duplexing
[e] CSMA/CA: Carrier-sense multiple access with collision avoidance
[f] TDMA: Time-division multiple access

– Heterogeneity: WBANs involve several heterogeneous sensor nodes with different sizes, functions, energy demands and sampling rates. Thus, QoS³ needs may vary from application to application.

3 Machine Learning

Machine learning is a recent technology which allows systems to learn from experience when it is difficult to directly program the relevant computer tasks [15]. Machine learning can be defined as follows [5]:

– "The development of computer models for learning processes that provide solutions to the problem of knowledge acquisition and enhance the performance of developed systems."
– "The adoption of computational methods for improving machine performance by detecting and describing consistencies and patterns in training data."

Fig. 3. Machine Learning Process

Generally, the machine learning working process includes five steps, as illustrated in Fig. 3. Once the data is collected, the pre-processing step cleans the data by manually removing incomplete, unrelated or duplicate data samples. In fact, the collected data can not be used sometimes directly as we can have some kinds of interference or noise of physiological signals of human, due to sensor erroneous values, environment disruption, etc. [16]. The next step is to build the model and finally, we test the built model. In Fig. 4, training and testing phases are detailed; the training phase allows optimizing the performance by adjusting the parameters of the algorithm.

Machine learning techniques may be classified into three main categories: Supervised learning, unsupervised learning and reinforcement learning.

3.1 Supervised Learning

In supervised learning, a labeled training set is employed to construct the system model. The trained step is done depending on the given input data and the output is derived accordingly. Machine learning algorithms approximate the

---

³ QoS: Quality of Service.

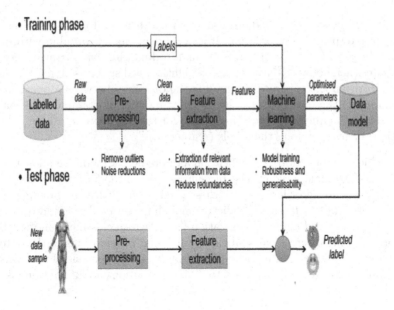

Fig. 4. Training and Testing phases [9]

relationship between the input data and the expected output. The process of supervised machine learning is described in [17].

Generally, supervised learning is performed in two manners, either by classification or by regression. Classification, a subcategory of supervised learning, aims to predict the categorical class labels of new instances on the basis of past observations. Regression, another subfield of supervised learning, seeks to model the relationship between a number of features and a continuous target variable. In classification, the input data is labeled with output tags, while in regression, the input data is mapped to a continuous output. The objective of both methods is to find patterns in the input data that can be converted into an efficient and accurate output. In the real world, it is not always feasible for data labels to be correct. Incorrect data labels can produce inefficient results and will evidently have an impact on the efficiency of the model. The most well-known algorithms are:

– Naive Bayes (NB): This is a probability-based statistical learning model, which assumes that all attributes are completely independent considering the class. In such a classifier, the learning agent constructs a probabilistic model of the features; based on this model, it can predict the classification of a new example [18].
– Support Vector Machines (SVM): It is a linear model for classification and regression problems. It can handle both linear and non-linear problems and performs well on many real-world tasks. The main idea of SVM is to create a hyperplane that separates the data into classes [19].

- Logistic Regression: A predictive analysis which is used to describe the data and to interpret the interaction of a dependent binary variable with one or several independent variables of nominal, ordinal, interval or ratio level.
- k-nearest neighbors (K-NN): It is a straightforward supervised machine learning algorithm that operates by finding the distances between a query and all examples in the data, picking the specified number of examples (K) that are nearest to the query, then casting a vote for the most frequent label (classification) or by averaging the labels (regression).

Machine learning, model classification and predictive modeling allow to build a model able to make predictions. In general, such a model involves a machine learning algorithm in order to make these predictions, it learns some properties from a given training dataset. Predictive modeling can be divided into two subfields: Regression and model classification [20]. Pattern classification models are built on assigning discrete class labels to particular observations as the outcome of a prediction. Regression models [21] are built on the analysis of relationships among variables and trends in order to derive predictions about continuous variables.

3.2   Unsupervised Learning

Unsupervised learning may also be called learning without teacher. In learning without supervision, the desired response is not behavior. Learning have to be accomplished based on observations. Appropriate mechanisms for self-weight adaptation must be incorporated into the trained network [22]. Unsupervised learning is known for its ability to find recurrent sequences of unlabeled activities of sensors that may include activities of interest [23]. Unsupervised learning is mainly based on clustering approach relying on grouping the unlabeled data into similar kind of clusters. Clustering constitutes a powerful solution in this context. However, some problems may occur during clustering, dimensionality reduction, missing data search, outlier detection, sensor failure detection and prevention [24]. For every problem analysis, many categories of algorithms were proposed. Thus, selecting the appropriate clustering algorithm for the each problem is a great challenge.

The objectives and the relative algorithms of both supervised and unsupervised learning in addition to reinforcement learning are exposed in Fig. 5.

3.3   Reinforcement Learning

Reinforcement learning involves taking appropriate actions to maximize a "reward function." With the reward function, we can penalize "bad actions" and/or reward "good actions". In reinforcement learning, the agent learns through interaction with its surrounding environment. Reinforcement learning is used by different software and machines to find the best possible path or behavior to adopt in a specific situation. The difference between supervised learning and reinforcement learning is that the training data contains the answer key,

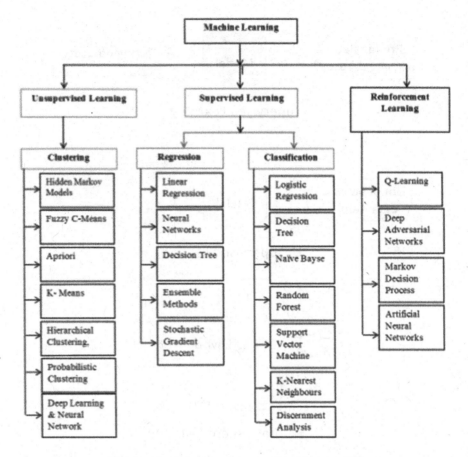

Fig. 5. Algorithms used in machine learning [25]

so the model is trained with the correct answer itself, while in reinforcement learning no answer is given, but the reinforcement agent decides how to perform the given task. In the absence of a training dataset, it is forced to learn from its experience [26]. Q-learning is one of the well-known learning techniques in which an agent regularly updates its rewards based on the action taken in a given state.

In summary, the three kinds of learning techniques as summarized as described in Fig. 6. Supervised learning refers to the machine learning task that consists of learning a function which matches an input to an output on the basis of examples of input-output pairs. Unsupervised learning is a machine learning technique where you do not need to supervise the model. Reinforcement learning is about sequential decision making.

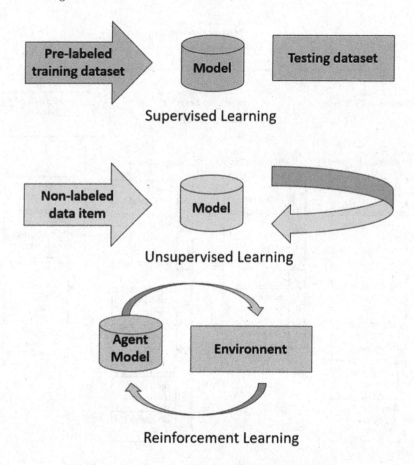

Fig. 6. The three categories of machine learning

4   Use of Machine Learning in WBANs

In the context of WBANs applications, the use of machine learning is required.
These kinds of applications deal with a huge amount of data. So, the processing of this high volume is beyond human capabilities; the physician's skills and
experience are too important to make a traditional diagnosis in many domains
of healthcare. Machine learning techniques can leverage a large volume of information to cover the full spectrum of diagnostic criteria of interest, allowing the
identification of reproducible markers, which can objectively stratify patients
according to risk [9]. For example, we can cite some machine learning-based
applications:

– Classification and analysis of diseases are the primary uses of machine learning in healthcare, especially for diseases which are considered difficult to diag-
  nose. Machine learning can help establish a rapid diagnosis based on the data
  collected.

– Personalized treatments are more effective by combining individual health and predictive analytics, they are also conducive to new research and better disease assessment. Instead of being limited to a specific set of diagnoses or estimating patient risk on the basis of symptom history and available genetic information, more information must be collected through devices or biosensors with sophisticated health measurement capabilities; this data can be leveraged by machine learning techniques to offer a personalized medicine.
– Machine learning can be used for system optimization by improving the data transfer, the energy consumption and the fault tolerance to cope with erroneous measurements and hardware failures [8].
– Machine learning can be used to understand the disease evolution of the patient, which contributes to enhance the patient health monitoring state [27].

Compared to supervised learning, which utilizes labeled data, unsupervised learning has neither labels nor a feedback signal. It is mainly applied to discover the hidden structure of data and to group them into similar clusters. It is mainly employed for descriptive modeling and pattern detection. A typical use of unsupervised learning in WBAN is anomaly detection. Thus, machine learning in WBANs is mainly used in prediction, classification, affinity and exploration, as illustrated in Table 2 [28]. In this section, state-of-the art approaches dealing with the application of machine learning in WBANs are surveyed.

Table 2. Machine Learning Objectives

	Supervised Learning	Unsupervised Learning
Classification	Decision Tree	Clustering (K-means)
	Neural Networks	Kohonen Networks
	Discriminant Analysis	Self Organization maps
	Bagging and Boosting Trees	
	Nadve Bayes Classifiers	
Prediction	Ordinary least	Not Feasible
	Squares Regression	
	Logistic Regression	
	Neural Networks	
	Decision Trees	
	Memory-Based Reasoning	
	Support Vector Machines	
	Multi-adaptive regression splines	
Exploration	Decision Tree	Principal components
		Clustering (eg; K means)
		Link Analysis
Affinity		Associations
		Sequences
		Factor Analysis

4.1   Supervised Learning Techniques in WBAN Applications

Activity Recognition. The provision of a system capable of automatically categorizing the physical activity performed by a human subject is of great interest for several applications in the area of healthcare monitoring and in the design of advanced human-machine interfaces. Figure 7 explains the process of human activity recognition (HAR) combining machine learning and sensing capabilities. The data collection step is composed of physiological signals, location of data, acceleration and environmental signals. The feature extraction step may be either structural or statistical. The feature

In the context of human activity recognition, the most common used classifiers are Bayesian methods, decision trees, Artificial Neural Network (ANN) and SVM. Accuracy, precision, recall and F-measure are the most performance metrics used to evaluate each selected classifier. According to [29], the most important metric for comparing the classifiers in activity recognition field is accuracy, development costs and computational requirements. For instance, SVM are generally used for pattern recognition in context-aware computing. It has been used to recognize patients activities in the healthcare domain. In [30], authors proposed a channel-based and topology-based methodologies for human activity prediction based only on the channel quality between the nodes placed on the

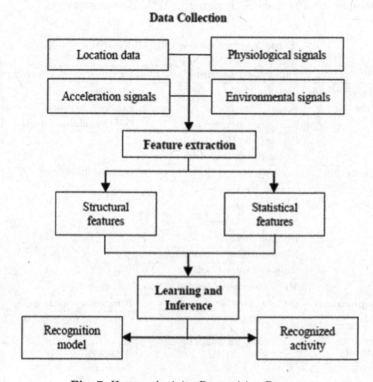

Fig. 7. Human Activity Recognition Process

body. In their experimental study, authors arrived to distinguish between three activities (stand, walk, run) with a higher accuracy while adopting supervised classifiers SVM, decision tree, random forest and LDA classifiers. Authors in [31] report 93% overall accuracy using SVM. Their approach based on 3-axis accelerometer and camera, were able to recognize nine activities. Similar work in [32], authors achieved average recognition accuracy of 92.25% with a tri-axial accelerometer in a trouser pocket and applying SVM classifier on four daily activities: standing still, jumping, running and walking. In [33], authors developed a software architecture able to perform activity recognition using wearable sensors. To achieve this, data sets for two users containing the stationary activities were recorded. Furthermore the data sets included non-stationary activities. Feature vector based identification and HMMs were used for classification and compared to one another. The goal of the system is to record the performed activities and location for later retrieval, in order to make the user's activity and location history searchable and see behavior patterns. HMM achieved over 90% accuracy for walking and walking with an umbrella and between 60% and 70% for climbing stairs, whereas feature vectors achieved between 60% and 80% on all other activities.

In [34], the authors also compared the performance of SVM, DCT[4], PCA, and SVM to recognize four daily activities: walking, jumping, running and standing through acceleration data. Employing kernel discriminant analysis, the objective of [35] was to distinguish stair ascent, stair descent, running and walking by retrieval and classification of accelerometer sensor data. Using Random Forest, the authors in [36] utilized motion sensors to identify some general daily activities like standing, walking or working on a computer. Authors in [37] got recourse to different classification techniques in order to predict human activities based on data analysis of wearable inertial sensors. Sensors were placed on chest, left ankle and right thigh. The activity recognition process includes three main steps: Placement of sensors, pre-processing and classification of data. In their study, authors considered k-NN, SVM, Gaussian Mixture Models (GMM), and Random Forest for supervised classification techniques. Classification techniques were compared based on the following metrics: correct classification rate, recall, F-measure, precision and specificity. For each classifier the input is the extracted features and the raw data. The results obtained showed that the k-NN classifier performs best compared to other supervised classification techniques.

Emotion Recognition. Generally, emotions are in fact recognized by analyzing videos recording audio (for voice/speech imprints), inertial signals (for hand gestures and body postures).

Most studies have used SVM as the basic classification model. Models like LBP[5] and K-NN have been employed to classify the features of various sensor data including facial expression, physiological data and voice to identify emotions such as joy, anger and sadness. In emotion recognition, multi-sensor fusion is

---

[4] DCT: Discrete Cosine Transform.
[5] LBP: Local Binary Pattern.

helpful for management of additional information. In fact, some emotions are more easily recognized by speech (fear and sadness), while others are recognized by facial expression (happiness and anger). Authors in [38] surveyed the majority or recent work on data fusion on the emotion recognition field.

Security. In [39], the authors proposed a temporal feature-based intrusion detection framework utilizing a temporal logic approach to detect Trojan and worm activities. The framework is based on supervised learning for classifying the monitored events.

Channel Status: Since a WBAN deals with vital signs that may affect human life, detection or prediction of channel status is required to ensure reliable communication between sensors. The authors of [40] presented a predictive learning based algorithm using NB method to efficiently predict coexistence conditions in a multi- WBAN environment. The proposed algorithm jointly applies packet reception ratio (PRR) and signal to interference plus noise ratio (SINR); these two parameters allow measuring the quality of wireless connections.

Medical Care Application. Authors in [41] summarized some machine learning approaches that have been employed for the detection of various major illnesses, including cardiovascular disease, Alzheimer's disease, diabetes. The authors of [42] found that algorithms such as naive bayes, K-NN, SVM, decision tree are the most commonly deployed in the case of heart disease prediction. The required data are collected from different body sensors, mainly blood pressure, heart rate, physical activity and weight. Authors in [43] proposed a framework for anomaly detection in medical WBAN for ubiquitous patient and healthcare monitoring. In this wireless environment prone to failures caused by the limited energy resources and computational power, the goal is to distinguish between irregular variations in the monitored parameters and to ensure reliable operations. To detect abnormal values (normal or abnormal), authors used SVM classifier. Once an abnormality is discovered, they apply a linear regression model; predicting values for each attribute in the abnormal instance is the goal.

To improve falls detection and prevention techniques, authors in [10] applied supervised learning to detect a specific type of patient movement in real time. This motion detection plays an important role in the evaluation of the daily activity of the patient to have a better and faster diagnosis. The authors considered the following attributes in their study: acceleration, time and motion class. The following movement classes were selected as they are the most relevant in daily human activities: Walking, running, sitting, jumping and falling. The authors of [44] presented a general methodology that is a combination of machine learning methods for the detection of changing temperature ranges of the thermal camera and adaptive image processing methods for estimating the breathing frequency. To identify individual temperature values, a neural network model is applied; the sigmoid and probabilistic transfer function are used in the first and second layers. Authors in [45] got recourse to machine learning techniques in order to enhance the performance of the fault detection mechanism in WBAN medical context.

In [22], the authors developed a system based on supervised ANN structure utilizing Fourier transform and windowed Fourier transform to detect ECG abnormalities.

In [46], the authors presented a method for arrhythmia classification; it was implemented on a digital signal processing (DSP) platform designed for online, real-time ambulatory operation to categorize eight heart rhythm states: Normal sinus rhythm (N), atrial fibrillation (AF), premature atrial contraction (PAC), left bundle branch block (LBBB), premature ventricular contraction (PVC), right bundle branch block (RBBB) supraventricular tachycardia (SVT), and sino-atrial heart block (SHB). The algorithm employs a wavelet transformation process with quadratic wavelets to identify individual ECG waves and generate a fiduciary marker array. Classification is performed using a probabilistic neural network. 17 ECG recordings gathered from the Physio Netrepository are used to test the algorithm. In [47], authors employed K-NN classifier to obtain an accuracy of 98.3%. Others work in the same focus adopted Discrete Wavelet Transform (DWT), Naïve Bayes and Random Forest methods [48]. However, these methods are relatively complex and are not suitable for a WBAN implementation; these networks are characterized by reduced processing capacity, limited storage and energy constraints.

4.2   Unsupervised Learning Techniques in WBAN Applications

Activity Recognition. Only few work adopted unsupervised learning in activity recognition. For instance, authors in [49] exploited unsupervised learning to extract and explore data gathered from accelerometers to predict the activities of humans. They also introduced a new performance evaluation method for classification. Authors in [37] got recourse to different classification techniques in order to predict human activities based on data analysis of wearable inertial sensors. Authors considered k-Means, Gaussian mixture models (GMM) and Hidden Markov Models (HMM) as unsupervised classification techniques.

Other Applications. Recently, the automatic detection of changes for monitoring of electroencephalogram (EEG) signals in real time has received great interest with a high number of clinical applications, as it shows the electrical activity of the brain; it is becoming an important way to record and understand the complex brain activities. Authors in [50] got recourse to unsupervised learning to detect automatic abnormal changes of EEG Signals in real time manner. Authors in [51] analyzed blood oxygen saturation (SpO2) for sleep apnea detection. Initially, they applied an unsupervised learning strategy to compute the initial weights. Then, they adopted a supervised fine-tuning in order to optimize the weights.

Authors in [52] used Hidden Markov Model (HMM) and Gaussian Mixture Models (GMM) for detection of a heart anomaly called Myocardial Infarction

(MI) using ECG signal with an accuracy of 82.5%. Authors in [53] proposed a channel allocation scheme for multiple WBANs to avoid interference between them. The proposed scheme tackles the problem of interference between several WBANs that are located side by side and are jointly sending and receiving information without any inter-WBAN scheduling. The channel allocation is performed by k-means clustering and vertex coloring algorithm using the location of WBANs and their mutual distances. The authors in [54] improved the clustering mechanism by employing unsupervised machine learning during the coloring process, taking into account the architecture and capacity of the WBAN equipment. UCA[6] algorithm is intended for spectrum allocation in multiple WBANs; it separates the nodes in the region by clustering, and the channel group is affected to the cells by coloring to realize the UCA. The authors, in [50], presented an unsupervised framework to automatically detect changes in the monitoring of EEG signals in real-time. The joint features of the time domain are first calculated to retrieve the temporal fluctuations of a given EEG data stream; then, they adopt a linear AR[7] model to model the data and calculate the temporal anomalies; finally, a nonparametric statistical test is conducted to provide an effective classification. A similar approach was adopted in [55].

4.3   Reinforcement Learning Techniques in WBAN Applications

Reinforcement learning is adopted in WBANs specially for designing channel access and routing protocols. To obtain a trade-off between the issue of inter network interference and power control problems in WBANs, a lightweight power controller was introduced in [56]. In order to enhance its performance, RL was exploited to control the transmission power level and to handle the internetwork interference. Only SINR[8] information is required; the BNC[9] node sends it towards the BN[10] node via a feedback channel. Authors in [57] proposed a novel algorithm for channel assignment in WBANs, noted RL-CAA[11]. RL-CAA interacts with the background in an unsupervised manner in order to choose the optimal frequency channel for the wireless sensor nodes. RL-CAA also considers traffic load conditions and attributes the optimal number of channels to meet the minimum throughput requirements of the system. A reinforcement learning-based routing protocol with quality of service support (RL-QRP) was introduced in [58] for WBANs. In RL-QRP, the optimal routing policy can be discovered through experiments and rewards, with no need to maintain accurate information about the network state.

---

[6] UCA: unsupervised coloring algorithm.
[7] AR: autoregressive.
[8] SINR: signal to interference plus noise ratio.
[9] BNC: Body Node Coordinator.
[10] BN: Body Node.
[11] RL-CAA: reinforcement learning - channel assignment algorithm.

5   Discussion and Open Research Challenges

Despite the fact that machine learning techniques have been applied to multiple applications in WBANs, many questions remain open and need additional research efforts. Due to the strict characteristics of WBAN environment, related essentially to the limited capacities of the nodes in terms of storage, computational resources and energy, the choice of the adequate learning technique has to be done judiciously. In [8], the authors enumerated the design factors that should be met when using machine learning in WBANs; we can cite among them:

- Energy: Models must consider the amount of computational and memory resources required to perform a prediction as this directly impacts the energy wastage in the process.
- Accuracy: Since people's lives are involved, a strict training and validation process must be followed to ensure that the model generalizes and can function properly in the unseen data while doing continuous evaluation and training to improve the model's performance.
- Scalability: As the volume of medical data is continuously increasing, it is necessary to implement an efficient storage and computing system.
- Reliability: For delay-sensitive WBAN applications, a fast response is required to act quickly and take the necessary preventive measures. Therefore, the inference time of the machine learning model is of great importance.
- Fault tolerance: Due to the internal or external factors, we may obtain wrong observations (abnormal behaviour, attack, etc.), machine learning techniques play an important role to ensure better fault tolerance and performance.

For example, in [30], we discussed the trade-off between the performance metrics such as the classifier prediction accuracy and the training time. For example, the naive bayes classifier is a supervised learning method based on Bayes' rule which exploits the computation of the posterior probability with prior information. It conducts classification by counting the number of examples. Naive bayes offers relatively small computational complexity when compared to other supervised learning methods (e.g., decision tree and neural networks) and can be easily deployed in detection devices [40]. Therefore, it can performs well in WBANs.

Generally, in terms of features kinds, SVMs and neural networks perform well when handling multi-dimensions and continuous features. However, logic-based systems behaves better when processing discrete/categorical features. On the other hand, in terms of samples size, for SVMs and neural network models, a large dataset size is needed in order to achieve the maximum prediction accuracy whereas a relatively small dataset is sufficient for naive bayes [17]. In terms of capacity of storage, naive bayes needs little storage space during both the training and classification steps, unlike the basic k-NN algorithm which requires a huge storage space for the training and execution phases. It also has been shown that k-NN is sensitive to irrelevant features which may not perform well in WBAN where the environment is usually unpredictable.

On the other hand, it has been proved that unsupervised learning methods cannot effectively carry out the estimation task in wireless networks in general, because of huge complexity of the algorithm and low estimation accuracy [40]. While considering error and runtime performances of all algorithms, random forest ensures the best performance for classification, while additive regression (with k-NN) performs best for regression tasks [43]. On the other hand, supervised learning algorithms are widely employed in wireless networks to estimate the variance of wireless resources and network environment. Reinforcement learning may be adequate to solve several WBAN issues such as channel issues due to the specific features and the dynamic aspects of the WBAN channel, discussed in our previous paper [59]. In pattern recognition, such as activity recognition, supervised learning is the most used. Finally, the choice of the better machine learning method depends essentially to the context of application, the WBAN capacities, the size of the datasets, etc. Based on their experiments, authors in [60] showed that the nature of the data, pre-processing steps and tune-up parameters play important roles in the final prediction. They found that all methods with careful tune-up parameters and good cleansing techniques perform very well (accuracy 94%) (Table 3).

Table 3. Summary of relevant work on WBAN using machine learning techniques

	WBAN Topic	Work	Techniques
Supervised Learning	Activity Recognition	[30]	Decision Tree, SVM, Random Forest, LDA
		[31,32]	SVM
		[33]	HMM
		[34]	DCT, PCA and SVM
		[35]	Kernel Discriminant Analysis
		[36]	Random Forest
		[37]	kNN, SVM, GMM, Random Forest
	Emotion Recognition	[38]	SVM, kNN, LBP
	Security	[39]	SVM
	Channel Status	[40]	NB
	Fall Detection	[10]	Decision Tree
	Rehabilitation Assessment	[44]	Neural Networks
	Anomaly Detection	[45]	Decision Tree, kNN, Random Forest Linear Regression
	ECG abnormality	[22]	Artificial Neural Networks
	Arrhythmia classification	[46]	Probabilistic Neural Networks
	Detection of anomaly	[43]	SVM, Linear regression
	Detection of a heart anomaly (MI)	[52]	GMM and HMM
		[47]	k-NN
		[48]	DWT, Random Forest, Naive Bayes
Unsupervised Learning	Activity Recognition	[49]	-
		[37]	k-Means, GMM and HMM
	Detection of interleaved patterns	[61]	-
	Detection of EEG abnormality	[50]	-
Reinforcement Learning	Channel issues	[56]	-
	Frequency Channel selection	[57]	-
	Routing Protocol	[58]	-

However, some challenges must be overcome for effective deployment of machine learning techniques [8]. In fact, predictive models are limited in the accuracy of predictions and are unable to be 100% exact all the time, which affects negatively critical WBANs applications involving human lives. Besides, the availability of well-populated public databases could enable evaluation and comparison of machine learning techniques to ensure reliable deployment later. However, existing databases are kept by teams or found on the web and contain few samples. Thus, the future medical systems will be able to monitor elder people as well as patients with chronic diseases remotely while they are in their own residential environments where they are most relaxed and comfortable, and to reduce expensive hospitalization costs and minimize frequent hospital visits. Thus, the use of machine learning techniques in the WBAN applications should mainly focuses on:

- Varieties and heterogeneity of Data: every day, each sensor device generates millions of data. Extraction and recognition of relevant and important information remains a challenging task, especially when the data is not structured.
- The need to improve the design of the existing communication models of data streaming for an efficient allocation of resources, process, and manage them for accurate recuperation of information on time.
- Cost-Effective Models: The future models for businesses have to provide good results with minimum cost and taking into account the available resources
- Real time Models: The learning models have to provide quick responses to the user on real time manner.
- Automation in Allocation of Services: The new business models should replace services provided by human with machine learning and big data analysts.
- Security: Ensuring the security of stored health data is also a key issue.

6   Conclusion

Wireless Body Area Networks are recent and active field which consists on several sensing devices which may be in, on or around the human body. These devices generate a huge amount of data which may deployed in several domains, mainly healthcare, entertainment and gaming and security. This big data require machine learning techniques for fusion, processing and interpretation. Since WBANs have strict challenges, the machine learning techniques adopted have to be applied appropriately. The following paper presents a road-map of the effective use of machine learning in the different WBANs research areas.

References

1. Negra, R., Jemili, I., Belghith, A.: Wireless body area networks: applications and technologies. Procedia Comput. Sci. **83**, 1274–1281 (2016)
2. Movassaghi, S., Abolhasan, M., Lipman, J., Smith, D., Jamalipour, A.: Wireless body area networks: a survey. IEEE Commun. Surv. Tutorials **16**(3), 1658–1686 (2014)

3. Manogaran, G., Thota, C., Lopez, D., Sundarasekar, R.: Big data security intelligence for healthcare industry 4.0. In: Thames, L., Schaefer, D. (eds.) Cybersecurity for Industry 4.0. SSAM, pp. 103–126. Springer, Cham (2017). https://doi.org/10.1007/978-3-319-50660-9_5

4. Yang, G.-Z. (ed.): Body Sensor Networks. Springer, London (2014). https://doi.org/10.1007/978-1-4471-6374-9

5. Cacciagrano, D., Culmone, R., Micheletti, M., Mostarda, L.: Energy-efficient clustering for wireless sensor devices in Internet of Things. In: Al-Turjman, F. (ed.) Performability in Internet of Things. EICC, pp. 59–80. Springer, Cham (2019). https://doi.org/10.1007/978-3-319-93557-7_5

6. Shalev-Shwartz, S., Ben-David, S.: Understanding Machine Learning: From Theory to Algorithms. Cambridge University Press, Cambridge (2014)

7. Rahmani, A.M., et al.: Machine learning (ML) in medicine: review, applications, and challenges. Mathematics 9(22), 2970 (2021)

8. Al-Turjman, F., Baali, I.: Machine learning for wearable IoT-based applications: a survey. Trans. Emerg. Telecommun. Technol. e3635 (2019)

9. Cummins, N., Ren, Z., Mallol-Ragolta, A., Schuller, B.: Machine learning in digital health, recent trends, and ongoing challenges. In: Artificial Intelligence in Precision Health, pp. 121–148. Elsevier (2020)

10. Horta, E.T., Lopes, I.C., Rodrigues, J.J.P.C.: Ubiquitous mHealth approach for biofeedback monitoring with falls detection techniques and falls prevention methodologies. In: Adibi, S. (ed.) Mobile Health. SSB, vol. 5, pp. 43–75. Springer, Cham (2015). https://doi.org/10.1007/978-3-319-12817-7_3

11. Farahani, S.: ZigBee Wireless Networks and Transceivers. newnes (2011)

12. Wong, A., et al.: A 1V 5MA multimode IEEE 802.15. 6/bluetooth low-energy WBAN transceiver for biotelemetry applications. In: Solid-State Circuits Conference Digest of Technical Papers (ISSCC), 2012 IEEE International, pp. 300–302. IEEE (2012)

13. Jovanov, E., Milenkovic, A., Otto, C., De Groen, P.C.: A wireless body area network of intelligent motion sensors for computer assisted physical rehabilitation. J. NeuroEngineering Rehabil. 2(1), 1–10 (2005)

14. Choquette, S., Hamel, M., Boissy, P.: Accelerometer-based wireless body area network to estimate intensity of therapy in post-acute rehabilitation. J. NeuroEngineering Rehabil. 5(1), 1–11 (2008)

15. Ullah, F., Islam, I.U., Abdullah, A.H., Khan, A.: Future of big data and deep learning for wireless body area networks. In: Deep Learning: Convergence to Big Data Analytics. SCS, pp. 53–77. Springer, Singapore (2019). https://doi.org/10.1007/978-981-13-3459-7_5

16. Kim, B.-S., Kim, K.-I., Shah, B., Chow, F., Kim, K.H.: Wireless sensor networks for big data systems. Sensors 19(7), 1565 (2019)

17. Kotsiantis, S.B., Zaharakis, I., Pintelas, P.: Supervised machine learning: a review of classification techniques. Emerg. Artif. Intell. Appl. Comput. Eng. 160, 3–24 (2007)

18. Wang, S., Jiang, L., Li, C.: Adapting Naive Bayes tree for text classification. Knowl. Inf. Syst. 44(1), 77–89 (2015)

19. Hasan, R.C., Ierodiaconou, D., Monk, J.: Evaluation of four supervised learning methods for benthic habitat mapping using backscatter from multi-beam sonar. Remote Sens. 4(11), 3427–3443 (2012)

20. Kumar, R., Kumar, M., Pandey, M.: Predictive modeling using supervised machine learning approach. Fire Saf. J. 104, 130–146 (2019)

21. Geng-Shen, F., Levin-Schwartz, Y., Lin, Q.-H., Zhang, D.: Machine learning for medical imaging. J. Healthcare Eng. **2019**, 9874591 (2019)
22. Thakare, R.D., Meshram, V.P., Chintawar, I.S., Patil, I.A., Nagrale, P.N.: DSP based ECG abnormality classification using artificial neural network. Int. J. 4(4) (2014)
23. Acampora, G., Cook, D.J., Rashidi, P., Vasilakos, A.V.: A survey on ambient intelligence in healthcare. Proc. IEEE **101**(12), 2470–2494 (2013)
24. Balakrishna, S., Thirumaran, M., Solanki, V.K.: IoT sensor data integration in healthcare using semantics and machine learning approaches. In: Balas, V.E., Solanki, V.K., Kumar, R., Ahad, M.A.R. (eds.) A Handbook of Internet of Things in Biomedical and Cyber Physical System. ISRL, vol. 165, pp. 275–300. Springer, Cham (2020). https://doi.org/10.1007/978-3-030-23983-1_11
25. Pandey, S.R., Ma, J., Lai, C.-H.: A supervised machine learning approach to generate the auto rule for clinical decision support system. Trends Med. **20**(3), 1–9 (2020)
26. https://www.geeksforgeeks.org/what-is-reinforcement-learning/
27. Yang, X., Dinh, A., Chen, L.: Implementation of a wearerable real-time system for physical activity recognition based on Naive Bayes classifier. In: 2010 International Conference on Bioinformatics and Biomedical Technology, pp. 101–105. IEEE (2010)
28. Obenshain, M.K.: Application of data mining techniques to healthcare data. Infect. Control Hosp. Epidemiol. **25**(8), 690–695 (2004)
29. Preece, S.J., Goulermas, J.Y., Kenney, L.P.J., Howard, D., Meijer, K., Crompton, R.: Activity identification using body-mounted sensors-a review of classification techniques. Physiol. Measure. **30**(4), R1 (2009)
30. Negra, R., Jemili, I., Zemmari, A., Mosbah, M., Belghith, A.: WBAN path loss based approach for human activity recognition with machine learning techniques. In: 2018 14th International Wireless Communications & Mobile Computing Conference (IWCMC), pp. 470–475. IEEE (2018)
31. Cho, Y., Nam, Y., Choi, Y.-J., Cho, W.-D.: SmartBuckle: human activity recognition using a 3-axis accelerometer and a wearable camera. In: Proceedings of the 2nd International Workshop on Systems and Networking Support for Health Care and Assisted Living Environments, p. 7. ACM (2008)
32. He, Z.-Y., Jin, L.-W.: Activity recognition from acceleration data using AR model representation and SVM. In: 2008 International Conference on Machine Learning and Cybernetics, vol. 4, pp. 2245–2250. IEEE (2008)
33. Ganti, R.K., Jayachandran, P., Abdelzaher, T.F., Stankovic, J.A.: Satire: a software architecture for smart attire. In: Proceedings of the 4th International Conference on Mobile Systems, Applications and Services, pp. 110–123. ACM (2006)
34. He, Z., Jin, L.: Activity recognition from acceleration data based on discrete cosine transform and SVM. In: 2009 IEEE International Conference on Systems, Man and Cybernetics, pp. 5041–5044. IEEE (2009)
35. Khan, A.M., Lee, Y.-K., Lee, S.-Y., Kim, T.-S.: Human activity recognition via an accelerometer-enabled-smartphone using kernel discriminant analysis. In: 2010 5th International Conference on Future Information Technology, pp. 1–6. IEEE (2010)
36. Casale, P., Pujol, O., Radeva, P.: Human activity recognition from accelerometer data using a wearable device. In: Vitrià, J., Sanches, J.M., Hernández, M. (eds.) IbPRIA 2011. LNCS, vol. 6669, pp. 289–296. Springer, Heidelberg (2011). https://doi.org/10.1007/978-3-642-21257-4_36

37. Attal, F., Mohammed, S., Dedabrishvili, M., Chamroukhi, F., Oukhellou, L., Amirat, Y.: Physical human activity recognition using wearable sensors. Sensors **15**(12), 31314–31338 (2015)
38. Gravina, R., Alinia, P., Ghasemzadeh, H., Fortino, G.: Multi-sensor fusion in body sensor networks: state-of-the-art and research challenges. Inf. Fusion **35**, 68–80 (2017)
39. Bose, A., Hu, X., Shin, K.G., Park, T.: Behavioral detection of malware on mobile handsets. In: Proceedings of the 6th International Conference on Mobile Systems, Applications, and Services, pp. 225–238. ACM (2008)
40. Jin, Z., Han, Y., Cho, J., Lee, B.: A prediction algorithm for coexistence problem in multiple-WBAN environment. Int. J. Distrib. Sens. Netw. **11**(3), 386842 (2015)
41. Chui, K.T., Alhalabi, W., Pang, S.S.H., de Pablos, P.O., Liu, R.W., Zhao, M.: Disease diagnosis in smart healthcare: innovation, technologies and applications. Sustainability **9**(12), 2309 (2017)
42. Almustafa, K.M.: Prediction of heart disease and classifiers' sensitivity analysis. BMC Bioinform. **21**(1), 1–18 (2020)
43. Salem, O., Guerassimov, A., Mehaoua, A., Marcus, A., Furht, B.: Anomaly detection in medical wireless sensor networks using SVM and linear regression models. Int. J. E-Health Med. Commun. (IJEHMC) **5**(1), 20–45 (2014)
44. Procházka, A., Charvátová, H., Vaseghi, S., Vyšata, O.: Machine learning in rehabilitation assessment for thermal and heart rate data processing. IEEE Trans. Neural Syst. Rehabil. Eng. **26**(6), 1209–1214 (2018)
45. Pachauri, G., Sharma, S.: Anomaly detection in medical wireless sensor networks using machine learning algorithms. Procedia Comput. Sci. **70**, 325–333 (2015)
46. Gutiérrez-Gnecchi, J.A., et al.: DSP-based arrhythmia classification using wavelet transform and probabilistic neural network. Biomed. Signal Process. Control **32**, 44–56 (2017)
47. Arif, M., Malagore, I.A., Afsar, F.A.: Detection and localization of myocardial infarction using k-nearest neighbor classifier. J. Med. Syst. **36**(1), 279–289 (2012)
48. Jayachandran, E.S., et al.: Analysis of myocardial infarction using discrete wavelet transform. J. Med. Syst. **34**(6), 985–992 (2010)
49. Machado, I.P., Gomes, A.L., Gamboa, H., Paixão, V., Costa, R.M.: Human activity data discovery from triaxial accelerometer sensor: non-supervised learning sensitivity to feature extraction parametrization. Inf. Process. Manage. **51**(2), 204–214 (2015)
50. Gao, Z., et al.: Automatic change detection for real-time monitoring of EEG signals. Front. Physiol. **9**, 325 (2018)
51. Mostafa, S.S., Mendonça, F., Morgado-Dias, F., Ravelo-García, A.: SpO2 based sleep apnea detection using deep learning. In: 2017 IEEE 21st International Conference on Intelligent Engineering Systems (INES), pp. 000091–000096. IEEE (2017)
52. Chang, P.-C., Lin, J.-J., Hsieh, J.-C., Weng, J.: Myocardial infarction classification with multi-lead ECG using hidden Markov models and gaussian mixture models. Appl. Soft Comput. **12**(10), 3165–3175 (2012)
53. Jiasong, M., Wei, Y., Ma, H., Li, Y.: Spectrum allocation scheme for intelligent partition based on machine learning for inter-WBAN interference. IEEE Wirel. Commun. **27**(5), 32–37 (2020)
54. Ma, H., Jiasong, M.: Improved unsupervised coloring algorithm for spectrum allocation in multiple wireless body area networks. Ad Hoc Netw. **111**, 102326 (2021)
55. Subathra, M.S.P., et al.: Detection of focal and non-focal electroencephalogram signals using fast Walsh-Hadamard transform and artificial neural network. Sensors **20**(17), 4952 (2020)

56. Kazemi, R., Vesilo, R., Dutkiewicz, E., Liu, R.: Dynamic power control in wireless body area networks using reinforcement learning with approximation. In: 2011 IEEE 22nd International Symposium on Personal, Indoor and Mobile Radio Communications, pp. 2203–2208. IEEE (2011)

57. Ahmed, T., Ahmed, F., Moullec, Y.L.: Optimization of channel allocation in wireless body area networks by means of reinforcement learning. In: 2016 IEEE Asia Pacific Conference on Wireless and Mobile (APWiMob), pp. 120–123. IEEE (2016)

58. Liang, X., Balasingham, I., Byun, S.-S.: A reinforcement learning based routing protocol with QoS support for biomedical sensor networks. In: 2008 First International Symposium on Applied Sciences on Biomedical and Communication Technologies, pp. 1–5. IEEE (2008)

59. Negra, R., Jemili, I., Zemmari, A., Mosbah, M., Belghith, A., Abdallah, N.O.: Leveraging the link quality awareness for body node coordinator (BNC) placement in WBANs. In: Proceedings of the 34th ACM/SIGAPP Symposium on Applied Computing, pp. 754–761. ACM (2019)

60. Awad, M., Sallabi, F., Shuaib, K., Naeem, F.: Artificial intelligence-based fault prediction framework for WBAN. J. King Saud Univ. Comput. Inf. Sci. (2021)

61. Ruotsalainen, M., Ala-Kleemola, T., Visa, A.: GAIS: a method for detecting interleaved sequential patterns from imperfect data. In: 2007 IEEE Symposium on Computational Intelligence and Data Mining, pp. 530–534. IEEE (2007)

Cyber Security of Connected Objects

Blockchain and Cooperative Intelligent Transport Systems: Challenges and Opportunities

Leo Mendiboure[✉][ID]

University Gustave Eiffel (COSYS/ERENA), Bordeaux, France
leo.mendiboure@univ-eiffel.fr

Abstract. Cooperative Intelligent Transport Systems (C-ITS) will play a key role in the advent of the automated and connected vehicle. However, C-ITS will have to be secured to prevent attacks from malicious entities and to provide the critical services required by connected vehicles (road safety). To guarantee this security, a solution that is widely considered today is the Blockchain technology. Indeed, this flexible technology, based on a decentralized architecture, could enable the implementation of innovative security services in vehicular networks. That is why, in this paper, we try to evaluate the potential impact of the definition of Blockchain-based solutions in C-ITS. To this end, we first propose an analysis of the C-ITS requirements and the Blockchain features. Then, we identify the potential areas of use of the Blockchain technology in C-ITS and we study the benefits/drawbacks of Blockchain for these applications. Finally, we present some challenges that will have to be considered in future Blockchain-based services designed for C-ITS.

Keywords: C-ITS · Cybersecurity · Blockchain · Data Protection · Reputation Systems · Consensus · AI · Green Blockchain

1 Introduction

Self-driving and connected cars appear as an interesting way to answer the main issues in the field of transportation: road safety, traffic congestion, etc. To coordinate with each other, these vehicles will have to exchange various pieces of information related to their position, their behavior (deceleration, lane change) or to the occurrence of external events (pedestrian, obstacle, etc.). This is why many industrialists and researchers are now working on the definition of Cooperative Intelligent Transport Systems (C-ITS), a transport system aiming to provide efficient and standardized communication between the different road users and the road operators [53].

A major challenge for these C-ITS, today, is cybersecurity [46]. Indeed, as this system is intended to provide critical services for road safety, it is essential

I. Jemili and M. Mosbah (Eds.): DiCES-N 2022, CCIS 1564, pp. 63–80, 2022.
https://doi.org/10.1007/978-3-030-99004-6_4

that communications between road users are secure. For example, without a sufficient level of security, a malicious road user (vehicle, roadside infrastructure) that would send erroneous information to surrounding vehicles could modify the behavior of these vehicles (deceleration, lane change, etc.) and could potentially provoke an accident.

To guarantee secure communications in C-ITS, both for data security (confidentiality, non-repudiation, etc.) and for data trustworthiness, a solution that is being strongly considered today is the use of decentralized systems, and in particular the Blockchain technology [43]. This technology, based on a Peer-to-Peer (P2P) network interconnecting independent nodes, aims to offer security services without relying on a central control authority. In a vehicular environment where vehicles could continuously exchange information, such a solution could be applied to provide security services as close as possible to the users without requiring a systematic use of the communication infrastructure. The programmability and the flexibility enabled by this technology could also allow the development of new global C-ITS services [35].

This is why many papers have already proposed solutions based on this technology in vehicular networks both to improve security and to imagine future services for transport systems. Different surveys present an overview of the different approaches that have already been considered so far in the literature [1,9,11,16,23,37,39]. However, unlike state-of-the-art papers, this survey aims to propose a description of the existing work more oriented towards applications (road safety, commercial, etc.) than towards security or Blockchain benefits. In addition, potential developments of the Blockchain in a large sense (beyond the borders of C-ITS), placed in the vehicular context, are presented. The main contributions of this paper are:

- an analysis of the C-ITS requirements and the Blockchain features;
- an identification of the potential areas of use of the Blockchain technology in C-ITS;
- a study of the potential benefits of Blockchain for these applications and the current issues;
- a presentation of challenges that will have to be considered in future Blockchain-based services for C-ITS.

The rest of this paper is organized as follows: Section 2 presents background information on C-ITS and Blockchain. Then, Section 3 introduces potential applications of the Blockchain technology in C-ITS and the benefits that could be excepted using Blockchain-based solutions. Finally, the main challenges related to the future deployment of Blockchain-based solutions in C-ITS are described.

2   Background

In this section, background information related to C-ITS and Blockchain are presented. The main objective is to identify the security requirements of C-ITS and the features of the Blockchain technology.

2.1 Cooperative Intelligent Transport Systems: Short Introduction

As noted in the introduction, C-ITS aim to provide global services for future transport systems (cf. Figure 1). These services should in particular enable to improve road safety (obstacles detection, safe lane changes, etc.), traffic efficiency (redirection of vehicle flows, live traffic information) and user comfort (streaming, e-health, etc.) by allowing vehicles to exchange information with each other and with other devices/cloud servers via a roadside infrastructure. Different papers deal with a presentation of these services such as [34,50,57].

Today, vehicles can exchange information with connected traffic control signs, connected lighting and potentially smartphones to locate nearby pedestrians and cyclists using On Board Units (OBU). These communications can now rely on various Radio Access Technologies (RATs) such as cellular networks (LTE-V2X, 5G), a WiFi standard specifically designed for vehicular communications (802.11p) through Road Side Units (RSU) or even Bluetooth for exchanges with surrounding devices. Various documents can provide information about these radio access technologies for C-ITS [29,41].

Our survey, and existing research effort on cybersecurity for C-ITS, focuses mainly on services for road safety as these services are critical and their security is therefore essential. However, other services (traffic management, multimedia, etc.) are also vulnerable to attacks and proposed solutions could also be applied in this context. The classical security solutions considered today in the vehicular environment are the use of a Public Key Infrastructure (PKI) and a Certificate Authority (CA) for both vehicles' certificates, users privacy and access control management. Such an architecture can guarantee both data integrity, confidentiality, non-repudiation and availability [5].

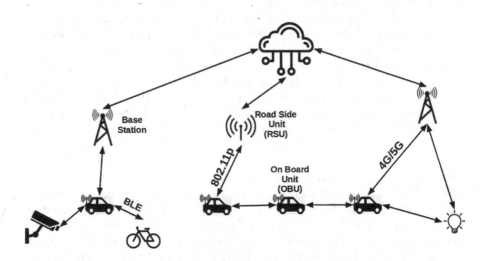

Fig. 1. Basic representation of the C-ITS architecture

Nevertheless, this reliable and well-known solution presents some limitations specific to centralized architectures, including, existence of a single point of failure, required Internet connection, complexity of information distribution [33]. Moreover, beyond information security and privacy protection, another question arises today in the vehicular environment: the verification of the reliability of the information exchanged between vehicles (trust establishment). Indeed, a malicious or corrupted entity, authenticated and with authorized access, could try to transmit erroneous information to the surrounding vehicles to force them to change lanes, change direction, slow down suddenly, etc.

This is why it seems essential today to design security services for C-ITS that 1) provide efficient authentication, privacy and access control mechanisms and 2) guarantee trust establishment between vehicles thanks to an efficient analysis of the exchanged data. Moreover, these services should take into account the different features of the vehicular environment, including a) the high mobility of vehicles and the short lifetime of communication links which imply low latency and low overhead, b) the ever increasing number of connected vehicles which implies the definition of a solution that can scale up and c) the coexistence of heterogeneous devices (vehicles, traffic signs, smartphones, etc.) which implies the definition of standardized and generic mechanisms that can be applied to different architectures.

2.2 Blockchain Technology: Short Introduction

The Blockchain technology (BC), a distributed ledger technology, is a new architecture for data protection that is being widely studied today [30]. Unlike traditional security solutions (PKI), BC is based on a decentralized architecture and a P2P network. With BC, each node of the network is involved in system security as a global and shared database (BC ledger) is maintained among all these nodes. This BC ledger stores all pieces on information exchanged between these nodes such as currency (typical BC application), certificates or other data structures. The BC nodes not only store this register, they also participate in its verification and evolution. Indeed, this BC ledger cannot be modified without the agreement of most BC nodes (51%). Therefore, BC allows to establish trust between nodes without them requiring to trust their neighbors: everyone is responsible for the security of the network.

In a BC architecture, nodes agreement and BC modification are based on a mechanism called consensus. This consensus aims to guarantee the stability and security (Byzantine general problem) of this decentralized system. The first implementable consensus protocol that has been proposed, during the development of the Bitcoin crypto-system [42], was the Proof-of-Work (PoW) algorithm (proof: performing a pre-defined computational effort). However, many algorithms have since been proposed and deployed [7]: Proof-of-Stake (PoS - proof: amount of crypto-currency locked up), Delegated Proof-of-Stake (DPoS - proof: scalable PoS), Proof-of-Authority (POA - proof: designated actors), Proof of Space, etc. Some articles like [44] offer an interesting and clear description of how Blockchain technology works.

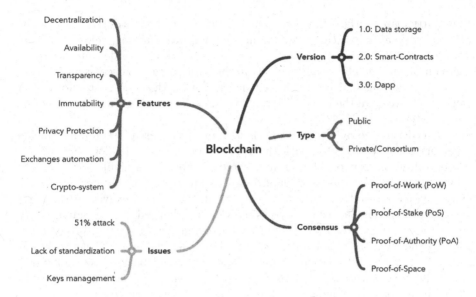

Fig. 2. Blockchain technology: Visual summary

Although BC is a recent technology, it has experienced significant developments over the past few years and several "versions" of the BC technology can be identified. Blockchain 1.0 corresponds to the first implementation of the BC technology. It has been designed during the development of the Bitcoin BC. The objective was to enable the exchange of crypto-currencies between BC users to propose an alternative to current bank systems. This version only allowed the exchange of data between the network nodes: crypto-currencies, certificates, etc. With Blockchain 2.0 was introduced the idea of smart contracts or chain codes. These smart contracts are computer programs deployed within the Blockchain ledger. Using these programs, two parties can negotiate the terms of an agreement, verify fulfillment and execute the agreed terms without a third party [33]. With smart contracts, Blockchain 2.0 is not only able to store data in a BC ledger but also to interact efficiently and securely with this data: modification of a value, addition/deletion of an element, complex operations, etc. Therefore, this BC version could be applied to various applications including advertisement and infotainment services. Finally, Blockchain 3.0 refers to the current evolution of the BC technology. An important idea of this version is the design of decentralized applications (DApp) [12]: besides efficiently processing data (smart contracts), the BC also provides a secure visual interface allowing the user to communicate with the smart contracts through a graphical interface. Thus, this new version of the BC is expected to allow its adoption by the mass market. The integration of Artificial Intelligence (AI) algorithms/tools in smart contracts could now be considered as a future direction for Blockchain 4.0.

BC can be based both on a public or private/consortium BC network. This means that, depending on the use case, the number/diversity of BC nodes that can participate in the BC network management can be restricted. In a public BC network, all nodes can take part in the information storage and verification process. In contrast, in a private/consortium network only nodes authorized by the consortium members can take part in this process and can access data. Thus, different solutions can be considered depending on the objective: information sharing between all the nodes of the network, exchange between a set of specific nodes, etc.

Considering the BC features and the BC underlying architecture, the benefits that are usually associated with the application of this technology are [37]: 1) decentralization that could guarantee the deployment of scalable security solutions ; 2) availability as a common ledger is deployed (and accessible) over a large number of nodes ; 3) transparency as all the nodes involved in the management of the BC ledger can access data within that ledger ; 4) immutability as data stored in a BC ledger cannot be modified : 5) privacy preservation as a pseudonym address is used to hide users identity in a BC network ; 6) secure exchanges automation as smart contracts could be used to deploy efficient resource sharing services and 7) crypto-system as crypto-currencies could be used to automate payments without incurring fees for the users.

Nevertheless despite these benefits, the BC technology still presents some limitations today [32,61], in particular, 1) the 51% attack, if a group of nodes represents more than 51% of the nodes in the network, it may take control of the network and corrupt its behavior ; 2) the lack of standardization as the technology is recent, its standardization at a national and international level has not been fully achieved yet ; 3) keys management as the signature of the chain of blocks by a large set of nodes (one block = one node) implies the storage of a large number of public keys.

3   Applying Blockchain in Cooperative-Intelligent Transport Systems

This section aims to present a set of information related to the application of BC in C-ITS: 1) potential application areas ; 2) expected benefits for Blockchain-based applications in C-ITS ; 3) current challenges related to this implementation.

3.1   Potential Areas of Application

As noted in Section 2, the characteristics of the Blockchain (see Figure 2) seem to be applicable to many areas in C-ITS both for non-commercial (road safety) and commercial applications (Insurance, healthcare, resource sharing, etc.) [1,9]:

- Secure road safety services: This is the main objective of C-ITS and probably one of the most interesting application areas of BC in C-ITS for researchers. As noted in the introduction, verifying the reliability of information exchanged between vehicles (crowd-sourcing, augmented perception) is crucial to provide secure and efficient road safety services. Defining specific BC consensus mechanisms for data analysis and data dissemination in C-ITS is an idea that is being widely studied today [22,40,58]. Moreover, such solutions could be applied not only to C-ITS but to many research areas requiring local data validation, without infrastructure: unmanned aerial vehicles, Internet of Things, etc.

- Insurance: Although insurance is primarily an economic issue, it can be linked to road safety with the BC technology. By storing all the exchanges between vehicles in a BC register, it could be possible to trace the exchanges and movements of vehicles in the instants preceding an accident (black box). Thus, in case of a litigation (forensics), it could be possible to clearly identify the culprit [15]. The application of smart contracts could also be used in this context to automate the compensation of road users when certain conditions are met (user data analysis);

- Identity management for connected vehicles: This is a third field of application that can be linked to the first two (road safety, insurance). This "passport for connected vehicle" is today promoted in the industrial, academic and governmental spheres [45]. Throughout its life cycle, a vehicle will generate a very large amount of information, such as administrative data (vehicle registration, resale, etc.), technical controls data, vehicle usage data (mileage, position) and driver behavior (insurance, road safety). The definition of a BC-based passport for connected vehicles could be used to store these different pieces of information in a secure and privacy-preserving way. This could also be used to allow the different players in the field to access the data relevant to them: manufacturers, administration, road operators, insurers, maintenance garages, etc.

- Road users healthcare - Users comfort: This fourth field of application is also frequently discussed in C-ITS. E-health systems could be applied to different situations including monitoring the vital parameters of vehicle users in real time or in critical situations (after an accident) or preventing the vehicle driver from falling asleep. In such situations, data exchange is still required with the infrastructure and with the emergency services. Therefore, BC could once again appear as a potential solution to secure these exchanges, guarantee the proper functioning of these healthcare services [32], and protect users privacy [60];

- Fee-based resources sharing : A final area where the application of the Blockchain could be interesting in C-ITS is the fee-based exchange of resources [4,10]. Indeed, whatever the type of business considered (video sharing, radio resource sharing, energy sharing, etc.), a payment must be made between the different actors. Blockchain could be very relevant in this context thanks to the use of smart contracts. Indeed, it could be possible to define, in a secure way, under which conditions the payment must be made and then to to verify if the conditions are fulfilled.

Beyond these existing applications that the BC could improve both in terms in security and scalability, this technology opens the door to new services that must be imagined.

3.2 Expected Benefits

Beyond investigating the potentials areas of application of BC in C-ITS, it also seems interesting to try to understand why researchers/industrial have decided to develop solutions based on this technology to overcome current challenges in C-ITS. Such an analysis is performed in this section.

Data Security This is the most obvious reason to apply BC in C-ITS as BC aims to provide a decentralized secure environment.

Users Authentication and Access Control. Regarding authentication and access control, the goal of a security system is to guarantee sufficient performance (latency, overhead) as well as a high level of security. Considering BC as a secure environment, researchers sought to demonstrate how this technology could significantly improve performance compared to classical PKI approaches by 1) deploying BC nodes, responsible for authentication and access control, as close as possible to the road users (roadside unit, base station) to reduce both communication overhead and latency [31] ; 2) by defining an efficient hierarchical architecture thanks to the flexibility of BC technology to provide optimal services [25] and 3) by proposing innovative handshake protocols guaranteeing important performance gains compared to classical approaches [26].

Availability. Data availability is undeniably one of the main advantages of BC: as the BC ledger is redistributed over a very large number of nodes, its availability seems to be guaranteed and many works have considered data availability as a fundamental assumption. However, some research papers, such as [56], focusing on scenarios without infrastructures and based only on ad-hoc communications, have tried to determine, in this context, how the BC could guarantee a high level of performance.

Non Repudiation and Integrity. These are also natural advantages of BC technology. Only signed and verified transactions are added to the BC ledger. It is then impossible to modify or delete these pieces of data (immutability), their integrity and non-repudiation are thus ensured. However, this could be problematic if intentionally erroneous or illegal data were added to the BC ledger, as it would then be impossible to remove it from the ledger [54]. The availability of data that should not be accessible is therefore a potential problem with this technology and is why some authors have raised this issue and proposed some counter-measures [2, 17].

Privacy Protection. In C-ITS, vehicles will be constantly exchanging information (Cooperative Awareness Messages - CAM - and Decentralized Environmental Notification Messages - DENM -) [47], so the implementation of mechanisms to ensure that they cannot be tracked (route tracking, behavior analysis, etc.) is essential. The BC associates a pseudonym to each user and thus seems to be a potentially interesting solution to improve privacy. This is why many authors have tried to develop this idea by proposing mechanisms for generating pseudonyms that 1) should only be used in a given geographical area at a given time [28] 2) should only be used during a communication session [49]. Some authors have also sought to improve the pseudonym generation process to provide a higher level of scaling (BC nodes selection) [59].

Trust Establishment. This is another potential application of the BC technology that could solve an essential problem in C-ITS: how can a vehicle be sure that an information is reliable when it receives it?

Data Reliability. To verify the reliability of a piece of information quickly, the most efficient approach seems to be to carry out this verification at the vehicle level or as close as possible to this vehicle. In this context, BC seems once again interesting: it can allow the deployment of local exchange networks between vehicles and roadside infrastructure to verify in real time that an information is reliable. To do so, the basic idea is to cross information coming from different sources (vehicles, cameras, etc.) and to verify that an information matches with the data provided by the other sensors. To do this, different BC consensus algorithms have been proposed in C-ITS, notably the Proof of Location and the Proof on Event algorithms [58]. These are used to ensure that a vehicle transmitting a message is where it claims to be and that it is not trying to hide its real position. In parallel, other works have also been interested in the scaling up of these verification systems through, once again, the definition of multi-layer BC networks: a local and fast verification can first be performed and a more global verification can then be imagined [52].

Reputation Systems. In addition to verifying the reliability of each message received, another way to establish trust between vehicles and to reinforce security is to implement and deploy reputation systems [19]. The idea behind these systems is to create a trust index for each vehicle and to modify this index according to its behavior: dissemination of erroneous information, non-sharing of critical information, etc. This could allow a vehicle receiving an information to quickly associate this information with a level of reliability: a vehicle with a low trust index will be more susceptible to send erroneous information that must to be verified. In this context, BC could also appear as a really interesting solution as smart contracts could be used to efficiently manage (storage, update, etc.) vehicles' trust indexes depending on their behavior [6,51].

Incentive Mechanisms. A final way to ensure trust in C-ITS, as an alternative to (or in addition to) the use of reputation systems, could be the use of incentive

mechanisms. An incentive mechanism consists of rewarding a vehicle for partici-
pating in the successful operation of C-ITS. For example, a vehicle that actively
participates in the data verification or dissemination process may be rewarded,
which may encourage more vehicles to act cooperatively. For such applications,
the association of the BC technology with the use of crypto-currencies appears
to be a clear advantage. It could therefore be simple to set up smart contracts
that would automatically remunerate vehicles. This is why many authors have
sought to define BC-based solutions for specific C-ITS use cases such as intersec-
tion management [52] or vehicles' crowd-sourcing [27]. Other authors have also
considered the use of existing BCs networks (Bitcoin in particular) to implement
vehicular remuneration mechanisms based on utility functions [3].

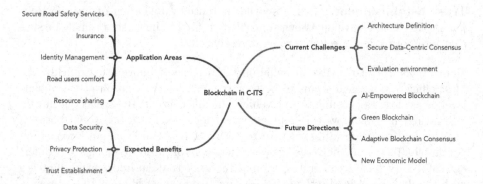

Fig. 3. BC in C-ITS : Visual summary

3.3   Current Challenges

The work currently being carried out by researchers not only aims to take advantage of the benefits of the BC technology. It also intends to adapt this technology
to the vehicular networks' features. Some of the ideas that are currently being
considered are presented in this section.

Architecture Definition. This is certainly the issue that is currently the most
frequently addressed. The definition of an optimal BC architecture is indeed a
major objective and the questions that arise today are numerous. A first essential question is to determine an optimal positioning for the BC nodes. Indeed,
vehicles, roadside infrastructure, cloud servers, and even other types of devices
(smartphones, IoT devices, etc.) could be able to host these Blockchain nodes,
and each of them has advantages in terms of computing/storage capacity, latency,
or management efficiency. It is therefore essential to determine which devices
should host Blockchain nodes and which applications should be considered. A
second key issue is to determine how the scalability of the BC network could

be improved to manage an ever increasing number of vehicles. In this context, many works are now proposing multi-layer BC architectures, composed of local BC networks and global BC networks as explained in [36], that could guarantee both low latency and high scalability thanks to a distribution of the processing load. However, the management of such systems would necessarily be complex. A last question that could arise, and that has been introduced in Section 2 of this paper, is the type of BC network that should be considered: public or private/consortium. This would have important implications on the type of nodes that could participate in the verification process and thus on both the security of the network (increased) and the transparency of its operation (decreased).

Secure Data-Centric Consensus. This is a second challenge that many researchers are trying to address today. The studies that have been developed in the last few years to reinforce the security of C-ITS have proposed adaptations of the BC that could enable its application in the vehicular environment (cf. section 3.2): mobility management, efficient pseudo-anonymity, specific consensus, latency, etc. However, some of these works, by focusing on the final objective (adaptation to the C-ITS requirements), have diverged from the fundamental security principles of this technology. Therefore, some consensus algorithms proposed for the verification of the information's reliability in vehicular networks are able to efficiently analyze data and to cross-check information coming from different devices but do not guarantee the security of the decentralized architecture as classical algorithms (PoW, PoS, etc.) do. This is why a major objective today is to define consensus algorithms adapted to C-ITS applications that also guarantee the proper operation of the BC architecture and the security of the data stored in the BC ledger [37].

Evaluation of the Proposed Solutions. This problem, although different from the first two (related to BC deployment in C-ITS), seems really important for the development of future BC-based services in C-ITS [38]. Indeed, there is currently no simulator/emulator/hardware-based solution designed for the evaluation of decentralized systems in C-ITS. Therefore, each paper relies on its own implementation and the comparison of these different solutions appears to be complex. The reliability of these assessments is also difficult to evaluate. This is why a major objective today seems to be to develop new simulation/emulation environments for this research area. To do so, it would seem interesting to consider tools such as Mininet-WiFi [18] which could allow, thanks to a Docker architecture (Containernet), to deploy real BC nodes and, thus, to provide a realistic performance modeling. Moreover, this tool can be associated with SUMO [24] which seems to be still today the most used tool for mobility simulation in vehicular networks.

4 Potential Future Directions

Beyond highlighting current challenges related to the integration of the BC technology in C-ITS, another point that seems important is the identification of future research directions that could be considered. Some of these potential directions are presented in this section.

4.1 AI-Empowered Blockchain

Artificial Intelligence (IA) tools (Deep Learning, Machine Learning, etc.) are now being promoted in many research fields and their application could also be interesting for BC and C-ITS [20]. First of all, these tools could be used to optimize the deployment of the BC architecture and thus guarantee high performance in C-ITS in terms of scalability, latency, etc. For example, these tools could be used to optimize the deployment of Blockchain nodes (optimal number and location), optimize inter-node communications/fault management and determine a real-time optimal length for Blockchain blocks [14]. It could also be imagined the use of artificial intelligence to choose optimal consensus algorithms to meet the constraints of specific applications (such as critical applications) [38]: latency, computing capacity, etc. Indeed, any algorithm is not necessarily adapted to any application. For example, PoW algorithms do not seem to be applicable to very low latency scenarios. Then, the next step would be to deploy AI algorithms in the BC network/ledger itself. This could lead to the development of AI-based smart contracts. Thanks to such an integration, it would be possible to carry out complex information processing within the BC ledger. This would guarantee 1) that the source code of the algorithms used could not have been modified by a malicious entity 2) that the origin and the level of reliability of the data used by these algorithms is known. Therefore, AI-empowered Blockchain could enable the deployment of secure and reliable AI services.

4.2 Green Blockchain

The environmental question and the reduction of the ecological footprint of IT/communication systems are major objectives today [21]. The first consensus algorithms proposed for BC architectures, in particular the PoW, induce significant energy consumption to maintain the system operation/sustainability. Recently, new approaches avoiding the consumption of computational resources have been designed for crypto-currency systems (cf. Sect. 2.2): PoS, DPoS, PoA, etc. However, these solutions do not seem to be suitable for the C-ITS applications mentioned in the previous sections: data reliability verification, access control, etc. Indeed, the operation of these solutions is associated with the exchange of crypto-currency. Therefore, the development of consensus algorithms that guarantee low energy consumption seems to be an important goal. Such algorithms have already been developed in other research areas such as Internet of

Things [8, 13, 48]. Another issue related to the BC technology is the storage of a very large amount of data on a large number of nodes. Therefore, it is necessary to define and implement mechanisms that would reduce the amount of information stored on these nodes and also limit the amount of information exchanged between then. The premises of such solutions are proposed in papers such as [36]. Efficient solutions developed to solve this issue could be applied to different research areas (not only C-ITS) and could also enable the deployment of BC nodes on devices with lower storage and energy capacity.

4.3   Adaptive Blockchain Consensus for C-ITS

This idea of adaptability is new being promoted in many research fields and BC should not be an exception. The main idea would be to adapt the Blockchain architecture and the consensus algorithms in real time according to different parameters: 1) the vehicular context (vehicles mobility, communication links lifetime, etc.); 2) the applications requirements (security, Quality of Service, etc.); 3) the user preferences (level of privacy for example) and 4) the vehicles capabilities (storage, communication, computation, energy, etc.). To achieve such a goal, different potential tools (fixed-time consensus algorithms, information prioritization, fair load balancing, etc.) and a generic architecture are presented in [38]. However, as also noted in this paper, there is still a lot of work to be done in this research area (BC nodes positioning, trade-off between applications requirements, vehicular context and vehicles capabilities, etc.) and the design of such a system could be advantageous to all C-ITS applications.

4.4   A New Economic Model

More than a future direction, this is one of the consequences of the emergence of the Blockchain technology and crypto-currencies. These digital currencies which can be exchanged based on automatic contracts, with a value that can be set by the BC ledger developers, open the door to new applications such as the fee-based direct exchange of information between objects in the Internet of Things [55]. Such applications can also be transposed to C-ITS. Beyond that, this new system that allows the exchange of data and money without requiring the use of a trusted third party, with low transaction costs and a privacy protection mechanism, could in the future lead to the development of new applications that could be based on an alternative economic system.

5   Conclusions

To enable the deployment of future Cooperative Intelligent Transport Systems, the definition of efficient security mechanisms is essential. To do so, one solution that is strongly considered today is the application of the Blockchain technology. Indeed, due to its properties (decentralization, flexibility, trust, etc.), this technology appears as an interesting way to deploy innovative security services in vehicular networks.

Therefore, in this paper, we focused on evaluating the impact that Blockchain could have on C-ITS. First, we highlighted the C-ITS requirements (mobility, need for trust, etc.) and the current progress of the Blockchain technology (smart contracts, Artificial Intelligence, etc.). Then, we identified potential areas of application of this technology in vehicular networks (road safety, resource sharing, e-health, etc.), the benefits associated with the application of this technology (data security, incentive mechanisms, etc.) and the current challenges (privacy, architecture). Finally, we have identified future challenges for Blockchain in the vehicular environment (green Blockchain, adaptive consensus, etc.). An overall conclusion of this paper could be that the interest given today to Blockchain in C-ITS seems legitimate and that many research works can be considered in this field for the coming years.

References

1. Aggarwal, S., Chaudhary, R., Aujla, G.S., Kumar, N., Choo, K.K.R., Zomaya, A.Y.: Blockchain for smart communities: Applications, challenges and opportunities. J. Network Comput. Appl. **144**, 13–48 (2019)
2. Aitsam, M., Chantaraskul, S.: Blockchain technology, technical challenges and countermeasures for illegal data insertion. Eng. J. **24**(1), 65–72 (2020)
3. Alouache, L., Nguyen, N., Aliouat, M., Chelouah, R.: Credit based incentive approach for v2v cooperation in vehicular cloud computing. In: Skulimowski, A.M.J., Sheng, Z., Khemiri-Kallel, S., Cérin, C., Hsu, C.-H. (eds.) IOV 2018. LNCS, vol. 11253, pp. 92–105. Springer, Cham (2018). https://doi.org/10.1007/978-3-030-05081-8_7
4. Andoni, M., Robu, V., Flynn, D., Abram, S., Geach, D., Jenkins, D., McCallum, P., Peacock, A.: Blockchain technology in the energy sector: A systematic review of challenges and opportunities. Renew. Sustain. Energy Rev. **100**, 143–174 (2019)
5. Aniss, H.: Overview of an ITS project: SCOOP@F. In: Mendizabal, J., et al. (eds.) Nets4Cars/Nets4Trains/Nets4Aircraft 2016. LNCS, vol. 9669, pp. 131–135. Springer, Cham (2016). https://doi.org/10.1007/978-3-319-38921-9_14
6. Awais Hassan, M., Habiba, U., Ghani, U., Shoaib, M.: A secure message-passing framework for inter-vehicular communication using blockchain. Int. J. Distrib. Sensor Netw. 15(2) (2019)
7. Bach, L.M., Mihaljevic, B., Zagar, M.: Comparative analysis of blockchain consensus algorithms. In: 2018 41st International Convention on Information and Communication Technology, Electronics and Microelectronics (MIPRO). pp. 1545–1550. IEEE (2018)

8. Bada, A.O., Damianou, A., Angelopoulos, C.M., Katos, V.: Towards a green blockchain: A review of consensus mechanisms and their energy consumption. In: 2021 17th International Conference on Distributed Computing in Sensor Systems (DCOSS). pp. 503–511. IEEE (2021)
9. Balasubramaniam, A., Gul, M.J.J., Menon, V.G., Paul, A.: Blockchain for intelligent transport system. IETE Tech. Rev. **38**(4), 438–449 (2021)
10. Bao, J., He, D., Luo, M., Choo, K.K.R.: A survey of blockchain applications in the energy sector. IEEE Systems Journal (2020)
11. Bendechache, M., Saber, T., Muntean, G.M., Tal, I.: Application of blockchain technology to 5g-enabled vehicular networks: survey and future directions. In: International Symposium on High Performance Mobile Computing and Wireless Networks for HPC (MCWN 2020). IEEE (2020)
12. Bogner, A., Chanson, M., Meeuw, A.: A decentralised sharing app running a smart contract on the ethereum blockchain. In: Proceedings of the 6th International Conference on the Internet of Things. pp. 177–178 (2016)
13. Chen, P., Han, D., Weng, T.H., Li, K.C., Castiglione, A.: A novel byzantine fault tolerance consensus for green iot with intelligence based on reinforcement. Journal of Information Security and Applications **59**, 102821 (2021)
14. Corea, F.: The convergence of AI and blockchain. In: Applied Artificial Intelligence: Where AI Can Be Used In Business. SC, pp. 19–26. Springer, Cham (2019). https://doi.org/10.1007/978-3-319-77252-3_4
15. Davydov, V., Bezzateev, S.: Accident detection in internet of vehicles using blockchain technology. In: 2020 international conference on information networking (ICOIN). pp. 766–771. IEEE (2020)
16. Elagin, V., Spirkina, A., Buinevich, M., Vladyko, A.: Technological aspects of blockchain application for vehicle-to-network. Information **11**(10), 465 (2020)
17. Florian, M., Henningsen, S., Beaucamp, S., Scheuermann, B.: Erasing data from blockchain nodes. In: 2019 IEEE European Symposium on Security and Privacy Workshops (EuroS&PW). pp. 367–376. IEEE (2019)
18. Fontes, R.R., Afzal, S., Brito, S.H., Santos, M.A., Rothenberg, C.E.: Mininet-wifi: Emulating software-defined wireless networks. In: 2015 11th International Conference on Network and Service Management (CNSM). pp. 384–389. IEEE (2015)
19. Gupta, M., Judge, P., Ammar, M.: A reputation system for peer-to-peer networks. In: Proceedings of the 13th international workshop on Network and operating systems support for digital audio and video. pp. 144–152 (2003)
20. Harris, J.D., Waggoner, B.: Decentralized and collaborative ai on blockchain. In: 2019 IEEE International Conference on Blockchain (Blockchain). pp. 368–375. IEEE (2019)
21. Imbault, F., Swiatek, M., De Beaufort, R., Plana, R.: The green blockchain: Managing decentralized energy production and consumption. In: 2017 IEEE International Conference on Environment and Electrical Engineering and 2017 IEEE Industrial and Commercial Power Systems Europe (EEEIC/I&CPS Europe). pp. 1–5. IEEE (2017)
22. Javaid, U., Aman, M.N., Sikdar, B.: Drivman: Driving trust management and data sharing in vanets with blockchain and smart contracts. In: 2019 IEEE 89th Vehicular Technology Conference (VTC2019-Spring). pp. 1–5. IEEE (2019)
23. Khoshavi, N., Tristani, G., Sargolzaei, A.: Blockchain applications to improve operation and security of transportation systems: A survey. Electronics **10**(5), 629 (2021)

24. Krajzewicz, D., Erdmann, J., Behrisch, M., Bieker, L.: Recent development and applications of sumo-simulation of urban mobility. International journal on advances in systems and measurements 5(3&4) (2012)
25. Lasla, N., Younis, M., Znaidi, W., Arbia, D.B.: Efficient distributed admission and revocation using blockchain for cooperative ITS. In: 2018 9th IFIP International Conference on New Technologies, Mobility and Security (NTMS). pp. 1–5. IEEE (2018)
26. Lei, A., Cruickshank, H., Cao, Y., Asuquo, P., Ogah, C.P.A., Sun, Z.: Blockchain-based dynamic key management for heterogeneous intelligent transportation systems. IEEE Internet Things J. 4(6), 1832–1843 (2017)
27. Li, L., Liu, J., Cheng, L., Qiu, S., Wang, W., Zhang, X., Zhang, Z.: Creditcoin: A privacy-preserving blockchain-based incentive announcement network for communications of smart vehicles. IEEE Trans. Intell. Transp. Syst. 19(7), 2204–2220 (2018)
28. Li, M., Zhu, L., Lin, X.: Efficient and privacy-preserving carpooling using blockchain-assisted vehicular fog computing. IEEE Internet of Things J. (2018)
29. MacHardy, Z., Khan, A., Obana, K., Iwashina, S.: V2x access technologies: regulation, research, and remaining challenges. IEEE Commun. Surv. & Tutor. 20(3), 1858–1877 (2018)
30. Makridakis, S., Christodoulou, K.: Blockchain: Current challenges and future prospects/applications. Future Internet 11(12), 258 (2019)
31. Malik, N., Nanda, P., Arora, A., He, X., Puthal, D.: Blockchain based secured identity authentication and expeditious revocation framework for vehicular networks. In: 2018 17th IEEE International Conference On Trust, Security And Privacy In Computing And Communications/12th IEEE International Conference On Big Data Science And Engineering (TrustCom/BigDataSE). pp. 674–679. IEEE (2018)
32. McGhin, T., Choo, K.K.R., Liu, C.Z., He, D.: Blockchain in healthcare applications: Research challenges and opportunities. J. Netw. Comput. Appl. 135, 62–75 (2019)
33. Mendiboure, L., Chalouf, M.A., Krief, F.: Towards a blockchain-based SD-IoV for applications authentication and trust management. In: Skulimowski, A.M.J.., Sheng, Z., Khemiri-Kallel, S., Cérin, C., Hsu, C.-H. (eds.) IOV 2018. LNCS, vol. 11253, pp. 265–277. Springer, Cham (2018). https://doi.org/10.1007/978-3-030-05081-8_19
34. Mendiboure, L., Chalouf, M.A., Krief, F.: A sdn-based pub/sub middleware for geographic content dissemination in internet of vehicles. In: 2019 IEEE 90th Vehicular Technology Conference (VTC2019-Fall). pp. 1–6. IEEE (2019)
35. Mendiboure, L., Chalouf, M.A., Krief, F.: Towards a 5g vehicular architecture. In: International Workshop on Communication Technologies for Vehicles. pp. 3–15. Springer (2019)
36. Mendiboure, L., Chalouf, M.A., Krief, F.: A scalable blockchain-based approach for authentication and access control in software defined vehicular networks. In: 2020 29th International Conference on Computer Communications and Networks (ICCCN). pp. 1–11. IEEE (2020)
37. Mendiboure, L., Chalouf, M.A., Krief, F.: Survey on blockchain-based applications in internet of vehicles. Computers & Electrical Engineering 84, 106646 (2020)
38. Mendiboure, L., Maaloul, S., Aniss, H.: Towards an adaptive blockchain for internet of vehicles. In: International Workshop on Communication Technologies for Vehicles. pp. 15–26. Springer (2021). https://doi.org/10.1007/978-3-030-92684-7_4

39. Mollah, M.B., Zhao, J., Niyato, D., Guan, Y.L., Yuen, C., Sun, S., Lam, K.Y., Koh, L.H.: Blockchain for the internet of vehicles towards intelligent transportation systems: A survey. IEEE Internet Things J. **8**(6), 4157–4185 (2020)
40. Mostafa, A.: Vanet blockchain: A general framework for detecting malicious vehicles. J. Commun. **14**(5), 356–362 (2019)
41. Naik, G., Choudhury, B., Park, J.M.: Ieee 802.11 bd & 5g nr v2x: evolution of radio access technologies for v2x communications. IEEE Access 7, 70169–70184 (2019)
42. Nakamoto, S.: Bitcoin: A peer-to-peer electronic cash system. Decentralized Business Review p. 21260 (2008)
43. Nofer, M., Gomber, P., Hinz, O., Schiereck, D.: Blockchain. Business & Information. Syst. Eng. **59**(3), 183–187 (2017)
44. Puthal, D., Malik, N., Mohanty, S.P., Kougianos, E., Das, G.: Everything you wanted to know about the blockchain: Its promise, components, processes, and problems. IEEE Consumer Electronics Magazine **7**(4), 6–14 (2018)
45. Rak, R., Kopencova, D., Felcan, M.: Digital vehicle identity-digital vin in forensic and technical practice. Forensic Science International: Digital Investigation **39**, 301307 (2021)
46. Sabaliauskaite, G., Cui, J., Liew, L.S., Zhou, F.: Integrated safety and cybersecurity risk analysis of cooperative intelligent transport systems. In: 2018 Joint 10th International Conference on Soft Computing and Intelligent Systems (SCIS) and 19th International Symposium on Advanced Intelligent Systems (ISIS). pp. 723–728. IEEE (2018)
47. Santa, J., Pereñíguez, F., Moragón, A., Skarmeta, A.F.: Experimental evaluation of cam and denm messaging services in vehicular communications. Trans. Res. Part C: Emerg. Technol. **46**, 98–120 (2014)
48. Sharma, P.K., Kumar, N., Park, J.H.: Blockchain technology toward green iot: Opportunities and challenges. IEEE Network **34**(4), 263–269 (2020)
49. Sharma, R., Chakraborty, S.: Blockapp: Using blockchain for authentication and privacy preservation in iov. In: 2018 IEEE Globecom Workshops (GC Wkshps). pp. 1–6. IEEE (2018)
50. Sharma, S., Kaushik, B.: A survey on internet of vehicles: Applications, security issues & solutions. Vehicular Communications **20**, 100182 (2019)
51. Shrestha, R., Bajracharya, R., Nam, S.Y.: Blockchain-based message dissemination in vanet. In: 2018 IEEE 3rd International Conference on Computing, Communication and Security (ICCCS). pp. 161–166. IEEE (2018)
52. Singh, M., Kim, S.: Trust bit: Reward-based intelligent vehicle commination using blockchain paper. In: 2018 IEEE 4th World Forum on Internet of Things (WF-IoT). pp. 62–67. IEEE (2018)
53. Sjoberg, K., Andres, P., Buburuzan, T., Brakemeier, A.: Cooperative intelligent transport systems in europe: Current deployment status and outlook. IEEE Veh. Technol. Mag. **12**(2), 89–97 (2017)
54. Staples, M., Chen, S., Falamaki, S., Ponomarev, A., Rimba, P., Tran, A., Weber, I., Xu, X., Zhu, J.: Risks and opportunities for systems using blockchain and smart contracts (2017)
55. Thakore, R., Vaghashiya, R., Patel, C., Doshi, N.: Blockchain-based iot: A survey. Procedia Computer Science **155**, 704–709 (2019)
56. Wagner, M., McMillin, B.: Cyber-physical transactions: A method for securing vanets with blockchains. In: 2018 IEEE 23rd Pacific Rim International Symposium on Dependable Computing (PRDC). pp. 64–73. IEEE (2018)
57. Wu, W., Yang, Z., Li, K.: Internet of vehicles and applications. In: Internet of Things, pp. 299–317. Elsevier (2016)

58. Yang, Y.T., Chou, L.D., Tseng, C.W., Tseng, F.H., Liu, C.C.: Blockchain-based traffic event validation and trust verification for vanets. IEEE Access **7**, 30868–30877 (2019)
59. Yao, Y., Chang, X., Mišć, J., Mišć, V.B., Li, L.: Bla: Blockchain-assisted lightweight anonymous authentication for distributed vehicular fog services. IEEE Internet of Things Journal (2019)
60. Zhang, A., Lin, X.: Towards secure and privacy-preserving data sharing in e-health systems via consortium blockchain. J. Med. Syst. **42**(8), 1–18 (2018)
61. Zheng, Z., Xie, S., Dai, H.N., Chen, X., Wang, H.: Blockchain challenges and opportunities: a survey. Int. J. Web Grid Serv. **14**(4), 352–375 (2018)

Blockchain-Based Real Time Healthcare Emergency

Thomas Lavigne[1], Bacem Mbarek[2]([✉]), and Tomáš Pitner[2]

[1] INSA Centre Val de Loire, Bourges, France
[2] Faculty of Informatics, Masaryk University, Brno, Czech Republic
{mbarek,tomp}@fi.muni.cz

Abstract. Healthcare Real-time emergency systems have attracted a great deal of interest from both academia and industry. It is important to provide timely medical services at remote areas through an effective communication between healthcare providers. The healthcare stakeholders (including the doctors, nurses, etc.) are facing tremendous problems to track the conditions of the patients, trace them, and coordinate their interventions. In several cases, the healthcare stakeholders are acting without or with little coordination since they do not have the same information about the patient. They do not have also the same trace about patient. In order to overcome these problems, we propose in this paper a Blockchain-based Real Time Healthcare Emergency (BRTHE-care) solution that will serve as a common platform for the healthcare stakeholders to provide immediate or real-time tracking and management of the conditions of the patients. The platform will also help Healthcare providers to interact with medical history records. Furthermore, we propose an intelligent agent to release the doctors from requesting updates about historical records and to help doctors in diagnosing disease. We run simulations using the Hyperledger Fabric Blockchain tool. Results show the efficiency of our solution in terms of communication failures, latency measurements, and the sending rates.

Keywords: Blockchain · Healthcare · Real-time

1 Introduction

In a modern healthcare environment, healthcare communication technologies are critical for connecting healthcare providers with their patients. Effective communication between healthcare providers and their patients should be trusted, timely, and secure [1]. In this context, the major challenges facing healthcare today is to monitor patient current health conditions and to provide immediate and real time coordination between healthcare stakeholders [2]. In particular, one of the promising technology for sharing and protecting vulnerable healthcare data is Blockchain [3]. Moreover, Blockchain needs to be established in healthcare applications in order to truly leverage the benefits provided by its distributed

© The Author(s), under exclusive license to Springer Nature Switzerland AG 2022
I. Jemili and M. Mosbah (Eds.): DiCES-N 2022, CCIS 1564, pp. 81–98, 2022.
https://doi.org/10.1007/978-3-030-99004-6_5

ledger to find solutions to problems in sharing sensitive medical records[4,5]. Due to the nature of the Blockchain, all patient personal data in the edge can be tracked in a synchronized and distributed blocks.

Although the current literature includes a rich set of Blockchain healthcare applications, such as [6,7], or [8], most of these are to control patients records, verify and protect healthcare data with Blockchain. While we consider that Blockchain is capable of controlling on real time the patient's health status. In this paper, we focus on the implementation of a new Blockchain that will serve as a common platform for the authority stakeholders to track the conditions of the patients, trace them, and coordinate their interventions. Moreover, Blockchain-based solution will permit access to patient medical history by using an intelligent Agent System paradigm to intelligently model healthcare diagnostic.

In the remainder of this paper, Section 2 reports on the existing works addressing Blockchain technology in the healthcare context as well as the Hyperledger Fabric and couchDB technology used as base for our work. Then Section 3 describes our proposed solution. Section 4 provides a thorough performance evaluation of our solution and the security features of the proposed solution are evaluated. Finally, Section 5 concludes the paper and outlines future directions for this work.

2   Related Work

Research in blockchain-based healthcare applications is relatively new but growing rapidly; so, a variety of Blockchain healthcare solutions have been developed with linked outcome to the distribution of healthcare data that can make patient information easily accessible to hospital and clinic patients. An interesting Blockchain healthcare framework is proposed in [7] to manage electronic health records using smart contracts in Blockchain. Using smart contracts, the framework is able to add in the blockchain the hash of the electronic health records, the access rights and data instruction associated to it for execution on external databases.

In [9], the authors have presented a Blockchain based solution in a mobile healthcare application to ensure data integrity and data management, while ensuring a tracability for the access. In [8], the authors have proposed PRE-HEALTH, a Blockchain solution to ensure privacy while sharing EHR (Electronic Heatlh Records). While providing anonymity and unlinkability, PREHEALTH prevents from querying personal data to avoid misuses and abuses. In [10], a blockchain-assisted secure data management framework (BSDMF) has been suggested for health information based on the Internet of Medical Things to securely exchange patient data and enhance scalability and data accessibility healthcare environment.

A solution using Hyperledger Fabric to manage HREs is proposed in [11]. The different healthcare stakeholders are included in the system, moreover, the solution aims to solve the problem of appropriate security, entrusted access control and handling privacy and secrecy issues in the healthcare system. In [12], the authors have proposed a Blockchain-based electronic healthcare record system for healthcare 4.0. Patients can add records and manage the access rights related to them for the other participants such as laboratories. In [4], the authors have presented DASS-CARE platform, a framework using Blockchain to solve multiple problems as standardization, or consent management, payment. In [13], an Internet of Things (IoT) sensor-based blockchain framework is proposed that tracks and traces drugs as they pass slowly through the entire supply chain.

Authors in [6] proposed a way to secure mobile agent in Blockchain for healthcare. The solution is to register the agent into the blockchain and to check for each request if the agent can be authentified and data integrity. The agent is blacklisted if it is considered as a malicious agent. In [14], authors propose an analysis of the performance evolution depending on the parameters in Hyperledger Fabric, such as the database type used. In [15], authors presented the benefits and also practical obstacles of the blockchain-based security approaches in IoT.

The development of a Blockchain based system ensuring real-time healthcare monitoring and tracking system with scalable network is required in order to ensure patients safety as well as transmission of sensible data. Indeed, as most of the healthcare solutions mentioned have the common drawback of being dedicated just to collect healthcare data generated across a variety of sources.

2.1   Hyperldeger Fabric

Hyperledger Fabric is a Blockchain Framework used to create a Blockchain network from scratch and to define a large number of the network parameters, such as organizations or chaincodes. An organization is composed of peer and authenticated by a couple private/public key, users are defined in the organizations and are authenticated like the peers. Organizations are connected to channels and can communicate through chaincodes on a smart contract. A chaincode is a set of functions that have to be used to interact with the smart contract related to it, a smart contract is a database model. Figure 1 sums up the main characteristics about Hyperledger Fabric, the Figure shows two organizations with two peers each connected to one channel and using on chaincode related to one smart contract.

The couchDB database is a database model that can be used in Hyperledger Fabric. Figure 2 presents how the ledger database is implemented in Hyperledger Fabric. This database is created in the peer and all the query or invoke operation are done in the peer. The couchdb database is different as it exists on its own through a docker. When data is query with a chaincode through one peer, a http request is sent to the couchDB docker. Then the database sends back a http response to the peer and the peer sends the information to the client. Figure 3 presents a scheme to explain how the peer is connected to the couchdb and how it communicates with it.

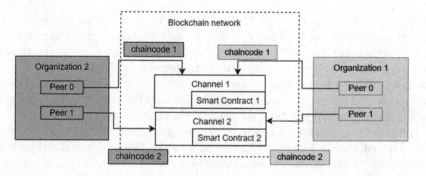

Fig. 1. Hyperledger Fabric example network

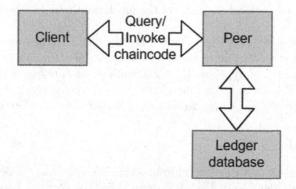

Fig. 2. Ledger database

The advantages of the couchDB database are that queries are easier to make. Indeed, we can query data using column tagname of the table such as in a SQL query.

3   BRTHE-care: Blockchain-Based Real Time Healthcare Emergency

In order to provide an effective distributed communications network for healthcare applications, we connect Healthcare stakeholders to Hyperledger Fabricbased Blockchain [16] to secure the peer and trust and use agent-based policy model to improve the Blockchain efficiency. The agent-based policy aims to reduce doctors interventions in the Blockchain, as the agent has the capacity to scan and to send a prescription request from a patient to their related doctor. Moreover, it helps doctors in diagnosing as it suggests drugs related to symptoms given by the patient.

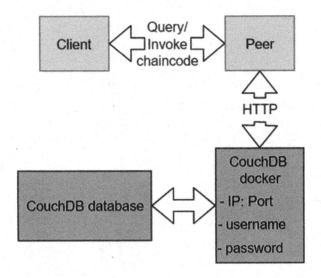

Fig. 3. CouchDB database

Our solution is a Blockchain network composed of six organizations and four channels which are described and presented, respectively, in Sects. 3.2 and 3.3, all organizations are granted specific rights for each channel. For example, doctors can create prescriptions but contrary to pharmacists they can't validate them. Figure 4 presents the general architecture of our solution and the rights granted for each organizations.

3.1 Overview of the Solution

Our solution manages the prescription, tests and history of a patient in a health-care system. Indeed, prescriptions can be created and validated, tests can be added and queried and steps of patients in the healthcare system can be recorded and queried in our solution.

Moreover, thanks to intelligent agents, patient requests for prescription are handled. Any patient requests are added into the network. When a new query is detected, intelligent agents will scan the request to know if their associated doctor should process it, in that case the request is sent to the doctor and add in the application database. The application can be a website, it is used to know the state of currently processed request.

The selected doctor will confirm or not the processing of the request. If no confirmation is sent before a predefined delay the application has to send the request to another doctor for processing till the request is processed. All steps are recorded for the request to know which doctor didn't confirm the processing or which one processed it. The confirmation is not enough and doctors have to close the request in the application after sending the prescription created. Doctors will check whether the prescription already exist or not and will search

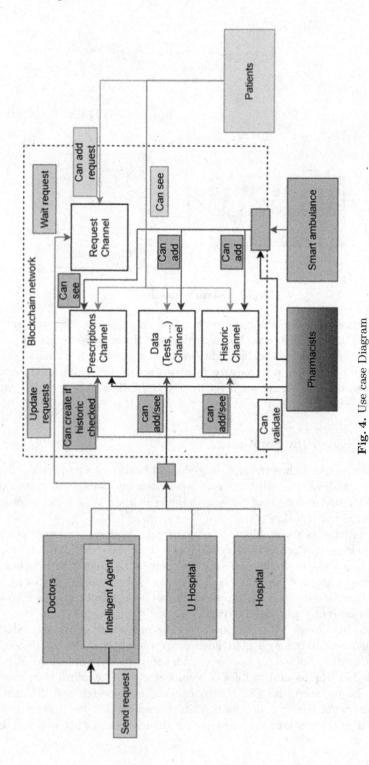

Fig. 4. Use case Diagram

in the patient history if the request is related to a medical appointment. A prescription is created if needed or an explanation is sent back.

Figure 5 presents the scenario above.

3.2   Organizations Details

The six organizations of our network are presented in the following paragraph. **Hopsital** and **U Hopsital**, which means university hospital, are similar organizations, Figure 6 and 7 present the different user types in these organizations. The user type student is added in the university hospital organization to give them special rights.

Doctors organizations contains all the doctors users, which are not in any hospital or university hospital. Each doctor has an intelligent agent associated and installed on their work computers, Figure 8 presents the Doctors organization.

Patients, **Smart Ambulance** and **Pharmacist** organizations are the last organizations and doesn't have special users.

3.3   Channels Presentation

In this part we describe all the channels of our solution, which are four in total: prescription, data, history and request channel. The first channel is used to handle and manage the prescriptions as it is composed of two chaincodes. The first chaincode smart contract is presented in Table 1.

Table 1. Class model for the chaincode 1, prescription channel

Prescription class model	
IdPrescription	string
DoctorId	string
HospitalID	string
HospitalServiceID	string
PatientID	string
Date, format D/M/Y	string
DrugsList	string
Details	string

Algorithm 1 presents the main functions of the chaincode, which are createPrescription to add the created prescription into the ledger. To query one by its ID the queryPrescription function is used.

The second chaincode is used by pharmacist to valid prescriptions, if there is no data about a prescription is the ledger then the prescription is still valid, for sure the prescription has to exist in the first chaincode ledger. The class model for validating prescription is presented in the Table 2.

The functions of the chaincode are defined in the Algorithm 2. The first function called validPrescription is used when a pharmacist want to validate a

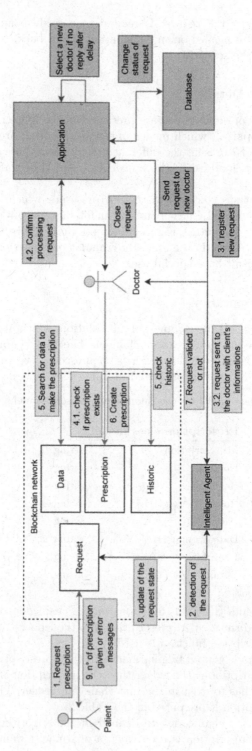

Fig. 5. Scenario of the intelligent agent when a patient submit a request

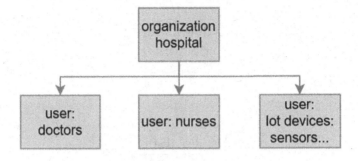

Fig. 6. hospital organization

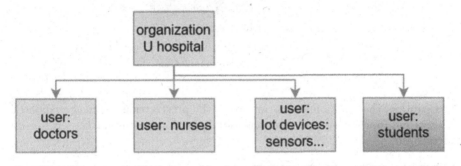

Fig. 7. University hospital organization

Algorithm 1: Functions for the chaincode 1 in the channel prescription

---

Function createPrescription(PrescriptionToCreate)
  return none ;
EndFunction
Function queryPrescription(IdPrescription)
  return Prescription ;
EndFunction

Table 2. Class model for the chaincode 2, prescription channel

Prescription class model	
IdPrescription	string
PharmacistID	string
Date, format D/M/Y	string
Status	string: "closed" or "invalid"
Details	string

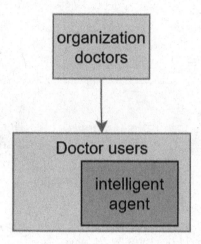

Fig. 8. Doctors organization

prescription, the function return an error if the prescription is already validated. The second function searchs a prescription by its ID, it is used to determine if a prescription is already validated.

Algorithm 2: Functions for the chaincode 2 in the channel prescription

Function validPrescription(PrescriptionToValidate)
  return none ;
EndFunction
Function queryPrescription(IdPrescription)
  return Prescription ;
EndFunction

The second channel is used to manage data related to patients such as tests made, the possible operations are querying and adding information into the ledger. The chaincode implements the model presented in the Table 3.

The second channel chaincode implements the functions defined in the Algorithm 3. The first function is used to create a test, defined in the test class model. To find a specific test using the test ID, the second function is used.

Algorithm 3: Functions for the chaincode 1 in the channel data

Function createTest(testToCreate)
return none ;
EndFunction
Function queryTests(TestID)
return Test ;
EndFunction

Table 3. Class model for the chaincode in data channel

Test class model	
TestID	string
GiverID	string
OrgID	string
HospitalServiceID	string
ServiceID	string
PatientId	string
Date	string
Results	string
Details	string

The third channel is used to keep the history of the patients into the healthcare system, as each steps are recorded into the channel. The chaincode will implement the model presented in the Table 4.

Table 4. class model for the chaincode in historic channel

Historic class model	
WorkerID	string
OrgID	string
HospitalServiceID	string
PatientId	string
Date format: M/H/D/M/Y	string
Details	string

Algorithm 4 presents the main functions of the chaincode. In order to have a tracability for each patient, the function addMoment enables healthcare worker to add a moment to patient history. To do so a historic class model is used as a parameter. To know a patient history in the healthcare system, the second function works with the patient ID and returns the history of the patient.

Algorithm 4: Functions for the chaincode 1 in the channel historic

---

Function addMoment(Historic MomentToAdd)
return none ;
EndFunction
Function queryHistoric(PatientId)
return Historic of a patient ;
EndFunction

The last channel is the request channel, this channel is used when a patient request a prescription from a doctor, the model for the request is presented in Table 5

Table 5. class model for the chaincode in request channel

Request class model	
RequestID	string
PatientID	string
PrescriptionID	string
WantedDoctorID	string
ListOfSymptoms	string
Date format: M/H/D/M/Y	string
Details	string
Status	string

The chaincode for the request channel is presented in the Algorithm 5. The first function is used to request into the ledger, the second one is used to query requests all request depending on their status, closed or open. The third one is used to query a request thanks to its ID. The last function is used to update a request status, to close it.

Algorithm 5: Functions for the chaincode 1 in the channel request

---
Function addRequest(RequestToAdd)
return none ;
EndFunction Function queryAllRequest(status)
return Requests;
EndFunction
Function queryRequest(requestID)
return Requests;
EndFunction
Function updateRequest(RequestToUpdate)
  return none ;
EndFunction

The Table 7 sums up all the rights of every peer or organisations for each chaincodes. The first column lists all the organisations that composed our network and the second one lists all the specifics users for each organisations. The abbreviations for the rights are in the Table 6.

Table 6. Abbrevations for the rights

Right	Abbrevations
Read	R
Write	W
Read and Write	RW
None	/

Table 7. Summary of the rights for each organisation and user

organisation	User	Channel prescription		Channel data	Channel historic	Channel request
		Chaincode create prescription	Chaincode validate prescription	Chaincode data	Chaincode historic	Chaincode request
Hospital	Doctor	RW	R	RW	RW	/
	Nurse	R	R	RW	RW	/
	IoT	/	/	W	/	/
U Hospital	Doctor	RW	R	RW	RW	/
	Nurse	R	R	RW	RW	/
	IoT	/	/	W	/	/
	Students	R	R	R	R	/
Doctors		RW	R	RW	RW	RW
Smart ambulance		R	R	RW	RW	/
Pharmacist		R	RW	RW	RW	/
Patients		R	R	R	R	RW

3.4 BRTHE-care Implementation

We have implemented a system prototype of the proposed BRTHE-care based on the open source Blockchain platform: Hyperledger Fabric [16].

Table 8 presents our testing environment variables, we tested our solution using Hyperledger Fabric version 1.1.0 and Hyperledger Caliper version 0.2.0 while running them on Ubuntu version 18.04. The characteristics of the virtual machine are that we throught VMware workstation pro we simulated one machine with 4 processors, with 2 cores each, and 8 Go of RAM.

Table 8. Details of the test environment

	Specification
Environment	Virtual on VMware workstation pro
Operation system	Ubuntu 18.04.5 LTS
Number of processor	4
Number of core/processor	2
RAM(GB)	8
Hyperledger	Fabric v1.1.0
Caliper	v0.2.0

As we are using intelligent agents to scan the request channel to find new request, we determined the algorithm of the agents. Moreover, the agents are able to propose a pre-diagnostic to the doctors to help them. The agents algorithm is presented in the Algorithm 6. The agents are multi tasking and have three main tasks. The fist one is **getNewRequest**, this function query in the request channel ledger the new requests, then the steps from the scenario are done:

adding the request in the database of the application, making a prediagnostic and sending the request to the doctor. The **getResponse** function is used when doctors have finished to process the request, it is used to update the request in the request channel. A check is done to know if the doctor has checked the history of the patient and the prescriptions related to him. If not, the agent ask the doctor to do it before closing the request. Finally the **newAssigment** is used when a request got a new doctor assigned, the agent will run the same function as in the **getNewRequest** part.

Algorithm 6: Agent algorithm

---

while *While True* **do**
    if *getNewRequests()* **then**
        for *request in requestList* **do**
            addRequestInDataBase() # step 3.1 in Figure 5 ;
            makeDiagnostic() ;
            sendRequestToDoctor(request.doctorID) # step 3.2 in Figure 5;
        end
    end
    if *getResponse()* **then**
        if *doctorHasCheckHistoric() and doctorHasCheckPrescriptions()* **then**
            updateRequest(requestRespond.prescriptionID, information);
            # step 8 in Figure 5
        else
            returnAskForCheck() ;
        end
    end
    if *newAssigment()* **then**
        queryRequest();
        addRequestInDataBase() # step 3.1 in Figure 5;
        makeDiagnostic() ;
        sendRequestToDoctor(request.doctorID) # step 3.2 in Figure 5;
    end
end

---

4 Performance Evaluation

To analyze the performance of our proposed BRTHE-care solution, we used Hyperledger Caliper software [17], which is a benchmark tool developed within the Hyperledger project. This tool can produce reports containing various performance indicators, such as transactions per second, transaction latency and resource utilization. For performance evaluation, this study is mainly focused on the communication failures, the send rate, and the average latency measurements.

We have run two tests for the performance evolution, which are detailed in Table 9. The table presents the parameters for the two tests in which we focused on the blockchain network and its interactions, we only tested the chaincodes functions, we have varied the parameter **tps** in our two tests, test 1 has a 50 tps send rate and test 2 has a 150 tps send rate. As the blockchain is the main part of the solution, it is important to know if it is reliable, efficient and scalable.

We tested our solution through one peer from one organization. The main variables are explained in the list below.

- **txNumber**: refers to the number of transaction to generate
- **rateControl type** refers to how the transactions are sent (linear, fixed rate, ...)
- **tps** means Transaction per seconds and refers to the number of transactions submitted to the solution every second

Table 9. Details of the test environment

Variable	Value for test 1	Value for test 2
organisations	2 peers	2 peers
Number of clients	1	1
txNumber	500	500
rateControl	type: fixed-rate	type: fixed-rate
	tps: 50	tps: 150

Tables 10 and 11 present the evaluation result of the communications failures, the sending rate, the Latency rate and the Throughput. The sending rate is the number of transactions submitted to the network every seconds, the Throughput is the number of transactions processed to the network every seconds. The latency is the delay between submission and process.

In the first test which is explained in Table 10, we configured the system with a fixed sending rate equal to 50 tps. In second test which is represented in the Table 11, we used a send rate equal to 150 tps. The main observation is that when we increase to 150 tps the send rate the average latency is twice more important for most of the functions, such as the **createPrescription** function for which the average latency goes from 3.98 to 6.17 s when the send rate goes from 50 tps to 150 tps.

Moreover, the queries request are slower than the writing request, the latency difference is closed to twice more important, for example for the **createPrescription** and the **queryPrescription** functions. The main drawbacks are the two functions **queryAllRequest** and **updateRequest** that have the same troughput rate in the two tests which means that the system is scalable but very soon limited. This situation is explained because for the **queryAllRequest** the chaincode has to check all the database. For **updateRequest** function, it is because it checks if the query exists or not, process the result and then update it.

Table 10. A summary of the results for test 1 with Caliper

Function's name	Success	Send rate (TPS)	Average Latency (s)	Throughput (TPS)
createPrescription	500	60.2	3.98	35.2
queryPrescription	500	60.1	5.40	38.1
validatePrescription	500	60.5	3.44	40.1
createTests	499	59.5	3.29	29.3
queryTests	500	60.3	5.24	38.2
addMoment	500	60.5	3.16	40.1
queryhistoric	500	60.5	4.68	39.4
addRequest	500	60.3	3.52	41.3
queryRequest	500	60.3	5.74	37.3
queryAllRequest	500	60.2	9.18	29.1
updateRequest	500	60.6	14.44	25.4

Table 11. A summary of the results for test 2 with Caliper

Function's name	Success	Send rate (TPS)	Average Latency (s)	Throughput (TPS)
createPrescription	500	159.9	6.17	55.4
queryPrescription	500	168.6	11.87	35.6
validatePrescription	500	169.1	5.43	53.9
createTests	500	170.6	5.70	56.2
queryTests	500	170.0	11.98	34.7
addMoment	500	130.7	9.45	39.1
queryhistoric	500	165.6	11.67	35.8
addRequest	500	158.3	5.94	53.6
queryRequest	500	169.7	12.26	34.5
queryAllRequest	500	168.2	14.84	28.0
updateRequest	500	170.0	17.14	24.8

4.1 Security Analysis

In this section, we present the security model and define the services offered by our approach. We guarantee the following security services:

- Our approach ensure authentication by using a certificate-based authentication. The framework uses certificate to prove every user or peer identity, the certificates use asymmetric keys. The certificate is generated by the organization administrator or the ordering service for each peer and users, therefore no identity abuses can be made as identity proof is necessary.
- Trust can be ensured using the endorsement strategy. When a transaction is submitted it has to be endorsed by endorsing peers, the number of endorsements needed depends on the chaincode policy. Thanks to certificates all endorsement are checked and then submitted to the ordering service, which will create blocks and add them into the ledger.

– Hyperledger Fabric uses the hash of previous block to link the blocks. Each block contains the hash of the previous block and the transaction. It guarantees the data integrity. Moreover, peers checks their own database by comparing it to other peers to verify data integrity.

5   Conclusion

In this paper, we have proposed a Blockchain-based Real Time Healthcare Emergency (BRTHE-càre). The BRTHE-care solution is mainly featured by integrating the Blockchain to healthcare application with agent embedded systems. In the BRTHE-care solution, we have modeled the agent to release the doctors from requesting updates about historical records and to help doctors in diagnosing disease. Furthermore, BRTHE-care has the potential to improve hospitals ability to control patient through the implementation and operation of a distributed ledger solution based on Hyperledger Fabric. In order to validate our solution, we have implemented the BRTHE-care solution in Hyperleder Fabric, and we have used Hyperleder Caliper to analyze the performance of our approach. The simulation results have shown the percentage of communication failures for transactions is very reasonable and implementable. It also shows that our solution is reliable and scalable in terms of send rate of transactions per second (TPS) and the average latency measurements.

As future works, we first plan to improve our model to make it more suitable in the real life by defining more organisations, for example adding the healthcare authority or the insurance companies. Further, we plan to add a payment channel to centralize payment. As the anti-collision system is one of the most important issue, we plan to develop an anti-collision routing protocol to solve this problem.

References

1. Jabbar, R., Fetais, N., Krichen, M., Barkaoui, K.: Blockchain technology for healthcare: Enhancing shared electronic health record interoperability and integrity. In: 2020 IEEE International Conference on Informatics, IoT, and Enabling Technologies (ICIoT). IEEE, 2020, pp. 310–317
2. Albahri, O.S., Zaidan, A., Zaidan, B., Hashim, M., Albahri, A.S., Alsalem, M.: Real-time remote health-monitoring systems in a medical centre: a review of the provision of healthcare services-based body sensor information, open challenges and methodological aspects. J. Med. Syst. **42**(9), 1–47 (2018)
3. Mbarek, B., Ge, M., Pitner, T.: Blockchain-based access control for IoT in smart home systems. In: International Conference on Database and Expert Systems Applications. Springer, 2020, pp. 17–32
4. Al-Karaki, J.N., Gawanmeh, A., Ayache, M., Mashaleh, A.: Dass-care: a decentralized, accessible, scalable, and secure healthcare framework using blockchain. In: 15th International Wireless Communications & Mobile Computing Conference (IWCMC). IEEE **2019**, pp. 330–335 (2019)
5. Mbarek, B., Jabeur, N., Pitner, T., Yasar, A.-U.-H.: Mbs: Multilevel blockchain system for IoT. Pers. Ubiquit. Comput. **25**(1), 247–254 (2021)

6. Alruqi, M., Hsairi, L., Eshmawi, A.: Secure mobile agents for patient status telemonitoring using blockchain. In: Proceedings of the 18th International Conference on Advances in Mobile Computing & Multimedia, 2020, pp. 224–228

7. Ekblaw, A., Azaria, A., Halamka, J.D., Lippman, A.: A case study for blockchain in healthcare:"medrec" prototype for electronic health records and medical research data. In: Proceedings of IEEE open & big data conference, vol. 13, p. 13 (2016)

8. Stamatellis, C., Papadopoulos, P., Pitropakis, N., Katsikas, S., Buchanan, W.J.: A privacy-preserving healthcare framework using hyperledger fabric. Sensors 20(22), 6587 (2020)

9. Liang, X., Zhao, J., Shetty, S., Liu, J., Li, D.: Integrating blockchain for data sharing and collaboration in mobile healthcare applications. In: IEEE 28th Annual International Symposium on Personal, Indoor, and Mobile Radio Communications (PIMRC). IEEE 2017, pp. 1–5 (2017)

10. Abbas, A., Alroobaea, R., Krichen, M., Rubaiee, S., Vimal, S., Almansour, F.M.: Blockchain-assisted secured data management framework for health information analysis based on internet of medical things. Pers. Ubiquit. Comput. 1–14 (2021)

11. Uddin, M., Memon, M., Memon, I., Ali, I., Memon, J., Abdelhaq, M., Alsaqour, R.: Hyperledger fabric blockchain: secure and efficient solution for electronic health records. CMC-Comput. Materials & Continua 68(2), 2377–2397 (2021)

12. Tanwar, S., Parekh, K., Evans, R.: Blockchain-based electronic healthcare record system for healthcare 4.0 applications. J. Inf. Secu. Appl. 50, 102407 (2020)

13. Singh, R., Dwivedi, A.D., Srivastava, G.: Internet of things based blockchain for temperature monitoring and counterfeit pharmaceutical prevention. Sensors 20(14), 3951 (2020)

14. Baliga, A., Solanki, N., Verekar, S., Pednekar, A., Kamat, P., Chatterjee, S.: Performance characterization of hyperledger fabric. In: Crypto Valley conference on blockchain technology (CVCBT). IEEE 2018, pp. 65–74 (2018)

15. Dwivedi, A.D., Malina, L., Dzurenda, P., Srivastava, G.: Optimized blockchain model for internet of things based healthcare applications. In: 42nd International Conference on Telecommunications and Signal Processing (TSP). IEEE 2019, pp. 135–139 (2019)

16. "Hyperledger fabric, https://hyperledger-fabric.readthedocs.io/."

17. "Hyperledger caliper. https://hyperledger.github.io/caliper/v0.2/getting-started/."

A Survey of Machine Learning Methods for DDoS Threats Detection Against SDN

Ameni Chetouane[1]([✉]) [ID] and Kamel Karoui[2] [ID]

[1] National School of Computer Science, University of Manouba, Manouba, Tunisia
chetouaneameni@gmail.com
[2] National Institute of Applied Sciences and Technology, University of Carthage, Carthage, Tunisia
kamel.karoui@insat.rnu.tn

Abstract. Software Defined Networking (SDN), as a promising network architecture, has the potential to replace traditional networks in terms of simplicity of network administration, programmability, and elasticity. However, due to the centralized control method of SDN, threats to system vulnerabilities can damage the privacy, integrity, and confidentiality of the system, reducing network security, performance, and efficiency. Distributed Denial of Service (DDoS) is considered one of the most significant cyber security threats to SDN. In this survey, we begin with an overview of the properties and architecture of SDN. We present the different threats against SDN based on which part of the SDN paradigm they target and which security aspects are affected, such as availability, integrity, and confidentiality. We also review the main recent works using Machine Learning (ML) and Deep Learning (DL) approaches to detect DDoS and discuss their strengths and weaknesses. Besides, we compare the existing methods based on their accuracy rate. Finally, we give an insight of future directions for DDoS detection in the SDN environment using the presented approaches.

Keywords: Software Defined Networking (SDN) · Network security · Security threats · DDoS · Machine Learning · Deep Learning

1 Introduction

Software Defined Networking (SDN) is the most discussed paradigm in the field of inter-networking technologies today. It is an open network architecture that has been suggested in the last few years to overcome some of the major shortcomings of traditional networks [1]. SDN proponents have stated that network control logic and network functions are two distinct ideas that should be separated into layers. As a result, SDN brought the concepts of control plane and data plane: the centralized control plane (the controller) administers the network logic and regulates traffic engineering activities, while the data plane (the

I. Jemili and M. Mosbah (Eds.): DiCES-N 2022, CCIS 1564, pp. 99–127, 2022.
https://doi.org/10.1007/978-3-030-99004-6_6

switch) simply handles the transmission of packets between networks [2]. Therefore, SDN can be considered as a centralized control system over a physically distributed switching infrastructure. SDN is intended for highly dynamic orchestration and QoS/security policy enforcement. In addition to SDN-related security applications and routing techniques, modern networks require a wide range of other features and policies, from traffic shaping to network virtualization, and personalized packet processing to Quality of Service (QoS). While SDN has many advantages, such as a highly scalable programmable interface for shaping network traffic, dynamic policy enforcement, rapid prototype development, and customized network service chaining, it also has inherent limitations and vulnerabilities, the most serious of which is control plane saturation (the centralised control) [3]. Although an SDN system must have multiple controllers, the failure of one controller would put the entire network at risk. In the event of a network controllers attack the entire network would be crippled. As a result, SDN is more vulnerable to DDoS threats than traditional networks.

In recent years, Machine learning (ML) and Deep Learning (DL) methods have gained significant prominence in the world of network security due to the invention of extremely powerful graphics processor units (GPUs) [4]. Various ML and DL methods have been developed for DDoS detection in SDN [5,6]. Both methods are effective in extracting meaningful information from network traffic and predicting normal and abnormal actions based on the learned patterns [7]. Besides, these techniques study attack patterns to identify them before network resources are exhausted. Defense systems can use machine learning approaches to detect Defense systems can use machine learning approaches to detect whether a particular user is a legitimate user or an attacker. In the first step, incoming network packets are inspected and added to the database using filtering policies. Selected features from the database are extracted throughout the feature extraction procedure (e.g., protocol name, port number). The selected features are normalized to increase the performance of the training process. The training step is performed using machine learning algorithms, which learn patterns from the data set. An incoming packet is classified as a DDoS attack or a valid user. The system then removes the discovered DDoS packets and modifies its filtering strategy to apply to the new incoming traffic in the final step.

Therefore, machine learning (ML) and deep learning (DL) techniques can give intelligence to the SDN controller, which provides a holistic view of the network by analyzing data, optimizing networks, and automating network service provisioning [8]. In other words, the learning capability allows the SDN controller to learn for itself how to make the best decisions in different network contexts.

There are many review papers that address ML/DL approaches in various disciplines. Little has been done about detecting DDoS in SDN using these methods. In [9], the authors presented a review of how to detect DDoS in Software Defined Networking (SDN) using Machine Learning (ML) and Deep Learning (DL) approaches. They compare the different approaches based on the accuracy metric. However, the review is not detailed enough and does not present the advantages and disadvantages of the presented methods. Aljuhani et al. [10] reviewed recent studies on DDoS detection algorithms using simple and hybrid Machine Learning approaches in modern network settings such as cloud, SDN, and IoT. However, the authors presented limited DDoS threat detection approaches and mainly concentrated on DDoS threat defense methods in various network contexts.

We present in Table 1 a comparison of our survey with the other existing reviews.

Table 1. A comparison of the paper with the other existing reviews

Survey	Years range	Architecture of SDN	Threats against SDN	Affected security aspects	Types of DDoS threats	Datasets	Advantages and limitations	Open issues	Challenges
Gupta et al. [9]	2016–2020					✓			
Aljuhani et al. [10]	2016–2020			✓	✓				✓
Our survey	2016–2021	✓	✓	✓	✓	✓	✓	✓	✓

In this study, we present the different threats to SDN while considering classification based on the SDN plane and interface with the affected security aspects. We also present an overview of the most relevant Machine Learning (ML) and Deep Learning (DL) methods used for DDoS detection in SDN. The contributions of this paper include:

- A classification of the different threats against SDN plane and interface with the affected security aspects.
- A comprehensive review of different Machine Learning (ML) and Deep Learning (DL) methods used for DDoS detection in the SDN environment including advantages and drawbacks. We reviewed the most relevant publications up to 2021.
- A comparison of the presented methods based on the accuracy rate.
- Challenges and some open issues are highlighted to provide insight on how to overcome problems in the SDN environment, as well as the limitations of existing ML/DL algorithms for DDoS detection.

The paper is organized as follows. Section 2 explains the research methodology. In Sect. 3, we discuss the properties and architecture of SDN. In Sect. 4, we illustrate the different threats against SDN. Section 5 presents the Machine Learning (ML) and Deep Learning (DL) methods used to detect DDoS in SDN. In Sect. 6, open issues and challenges are discussed. Finally, Sect. 7 gives the conclusion.

2   Research Methodology

The purpose of this survey is to present the different threats against SDN based on the SDN plane and interface and to identify important existing research related to DDoS detection in the SDN environment using Machine Learning and Deep Learning methods in order to synthesize their respective contributions in this regard. The flow chart of the survey is illustrated in Fig. 1.

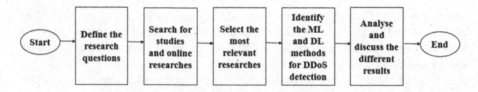

Fig. 1. A summary flow chart of the Survey

First, we have illustrated a list of research questions:

- What is Software Defined Networking?
- What are the different threats to SDN?
- What is the most significant threat to SDN?
- What are the different Machine Learning methods used for DDoS detection in SDN environment?
- What are their advantages and limitations?

Obviously, many other questions can be asked, but these ones should be sufficient to cover a wide range of studies. In the second step, we performed our study using the databases IEEE, Springer, Wiley, and Science Direct. The following keywords were employed: "Software Defined Networking", "security threats", "threat detection", "Machine Learning methods", "Deep Learning methods", "DDoS threat detection". These search terms were also combined to narrow the scope of the survey. We compiled a list of articles describing various risks to SDN, studies using Machine Learning approaches for DDoS detection in the SDN environment, and surveys on the topic, as well as the most recent publications up to 2021.

3   Software Defined Network (SDN)

Software Defined Network (SDN) is a kind of emerging architecture that aims to make networks more adaptable and cost-effective. It's an architectural strategy that ties the interaction between applications, network services, and devices, whether real or virtualized, to improve and simplify network operations [11]. The main characteristics of the SDN are as follows:

- The decoupling of the data forwarding plane and the control plane.
- A logically centralized controller that communicates with the data plane using open and established protocols and interfaces.
- Control applications that run on top of the element provide a network-wide perspective based on the abstraction of the distributed network state.

"Thus, software Defined Networking (SDN) is a centralized software-centric control over forwarding hardware". The decoupling of data forwarding and control planes enhance programmability of network control and applications [12]. SDN architecture may be separated into three planes: the data forwarding plane, the control plane, and the application plane, as illustrated in Fig. 2.

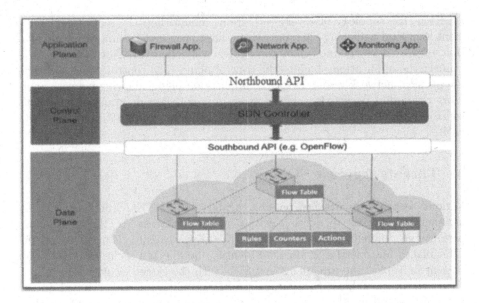

Fig. 2. The SDN architecture [13]

3.1   Data Forwarding Plane

In the data forwarding plane, wired or wireless media connects a large number of SDN switches. The SDN switches are responsible for the transmission of network packets. Each switch has a forwarding table, known as the Flow Table, that includes thousands of rules [14]. Rules are pushed down from the control layer by the controller, rather than generated by the switch node itself. It is worth remembering that the forwarding rule elements are pushed from the controller to the switch.

3.2   Control Plane

The control plane is the brain of the SDN; it administers and controls the entire network [15]. The SDN controller is the network node that implements these features, and it is typically installed as a distinct physical device with particular software. It tells the data plane whether or not to forward or change flows. The controller is also in charge of converting application commands into the lower-level communication protocol utilized by data plane devices. The first standard communication interface is OpenFlow, which is defined between the control and forwarding planes of an SDN architecture. It was created with a single controller, but this creates a potential single point of failure.

3.3   Application Plane

The application plane enables network operators to quickly respond to a wide range of business needs. Various application requirements, such as network virtualization [16], topology discovery [17], traffic monitoring [18], security enhancement [19], load balancing [20], and others, have been met by innovative application software developed to run on top of SDN controllers [21]. North-bound APIs connect the application plane to the control plane. The control plane abstracts the physical network resources for the application plane, allowing network operators to modify packet data paths using only software programming on SDN controllers, rather than individually configuring all physical switches in the data path.

4   Threats Against SDN

Various security threats are possible against an SDN environment that an attacker can employ to develop several types of attacks. In this section, we present the different threats against SDN and we classify them based on the SDN planes and interfaces, then we identify the affected security aspects. We present in Table 2 the threats against SDN with the target security aspects.

As shown in Table 2, threats against SDN could be classified based on the SDN planes and interfaces. These threats have greater destructive effects than simple networks and affect several aspects of security, such as availability, confidentiality, and integrity. SDN applications running in the application plane face significant security risks due to the lack of a defined security framework. These threats target confidentiality and integrity. Therefore, required procedures must be designed to establish a trust relationship between the controller and the applications running on it. In addition, a network application verification mechanism must be presented. The fraudulent flow rules threats in the northbound API interface affect the availability. This will lead to false rules in the network and packet loss. Therefore, a secure connection must be created between controllers and applications by implementing permission and authentication protocols [29]. Threats in the control plane target the three security attributes such as availability, integrity, and confidentiality. DoS and DDoS threats have an impact on the availability and security aspects. These threats may adversely affect the operation of the entire network, and the controller will not be able to respond to legitimate requests. Thus, the controller must be secure, and the use of multiple controllers is recommended. Threats against the southbound API interface have an impact on the availability and confidentiality security aspects. Man-in-the-middle (MITM) threat targets confidentiality and integrity. This threat type will have an impact on both the control and data planes. In this instance, the attacker may be able to change the flow of the switches or introduce new flow rules [29]. Therefore, mutual authentication can be accomplished by exchanging certificates between controllers and switches that are in charge of network packet transmission. Threats on the data plane are similar to traditional threats and affect the three security aspects.

Table 2. Summary of threats against SDN

Surface	Threat	Threat description	Affected security aspect		
			Availability	Confidentiality	Integrity
Application plane	Unauthorized applications [22]	The attacker can use programs that allow unauthorized access to get access to network resources and modify network operation		✓	✓
	Security rules and configuration conflict [23]	Conflicts between security rules can arise due to application complexity, leading to confusion of network services and management complexity		✓	✓
Northbound API interface	Fraudulent flow rules [24]	Malicious applications can introduce false rules into the flow table of switches		✓	✓
Control plane	Controller hijacking [25]	The attacker obtained sensitive information and has the ability to update any information and redirect traffic to any destination		✓	✓
	DoS/DDoS [23]	An attack on an SDN-enabled network can cause massive flooding in a short amount of time using their own host or manage other dispersed zombie hosts	✓		
	Unauthorized controller access [24]	Vulnerabilities in the controller can have effects that potentially putting the entire network at risk	✓	✓	
	Network manipulation [25]	The controller is compromised by an attacker who creates false data on the network, and then launches various network attacks		✓	✓
	Tampering [25]	The attacker instantiates new streams at the controller and permits activity to pass across the SDN and bypass security arrangements			✓
Southbound API interface	Man In The Middle [23]	It intercepts and modifies the forwarding rules sent to the switch, allowing control over the forwarding packets		✓	✓
	Black hole [23]	A malicious node presents itself as having the shortest route to the destination node	✓	✓	
	Network monitoring [26]	The attacker tries to learn the data transfer between the switches and controllers by observing the southbound interface		✓	
	Traffic analysis [27]	The hacker can gain access to important information by sniffing the packets sent to the switch	✓	✓	
Data plane	DoS [28]	In a flow table, an attacker sends a large number of packets to unidentified hosts in a short period of time	✓		
	Side channel [26]	An attacker creates a stream of timing probes (ARP requests for the MAC layer) and sends them to the OpenFlow network along with some baseline packets with known effects		✓	
	Topology poisoning [28]	To poison the global information acquired by a controller, topology poisoning threats forge or relay some control packets (i.e. LLDP) in an OpenFlow network	✓		✓

5   Detecting DDoS Threats Against SDN

Distributed denial of service (DDoS) is the most prevalent cyber threat that results in the depletion of system resources and, consequently, the unavailability of services to meet legitimate requests [30]. These threats are more harmful to SDN [3]. A successful DDoS attack can deplete the processor or memory of the SDN controller, resulting in network service interruption. Besides, DDoS threats can flood the secure south-bound channel by sending a large number of false requests, ostensibly from switches, causing the entire network to fail [31]. In this section, we first present the vulnerabilities in SDN and the different types of DDoS. Then, we present relevant work used for DDoS threat detection in the SDN environment and we focus on Machine Learning (ML) methods. We classify these methods into two categories: Machine Learning (ML) based methods and Deep Learning (DL) based methods.

5.1   Vulnerabilities in SDN

In this section, we present the vulnerabilities in SDN that make it highly vulnerable to DDoS threats.

SDN introduces additional risks of DDoS attacks by separating the control plane from the data plane. Besides, the OpenFlow protocol is used by SDN to communicate between the controller and its switches. OpenFlow introduces vulnerabilities to network assaults, particularly Distributed Denial of Service (DDoS) attacks [32]. When a switch receives a new packet in an OpenFlow-based SDN, for example, it first checks whether a flow rule installed in its Ternary Content Addressable Memory (TCAM) flow table matches the packet. The packet is forwarded by the flow rule if a match is found. If not, the switch buffers the packet and sends a message requesting a new flow rule to the controller. The controller then sends a flow modulation message to all relevant switches with the rules, asking them to process this new packet. This SDN functionality can be used by an attacker to perform a DDoS attack against the switch, the data channel interface, and the controller.

In addition, the backbone of network services is the centralized control plane, which is directly related to the availability, reliability, and data security of network services. Compared to traditional networks, the SDN controller is a critical point of vulnerability, and it is the first issue to be addressed in SDN security [33]. As a result, the control plane is vulnerable to DDoS attacks.

5.2   Types of DDoS Attacks

A DDoS attack is a well-known malicious attempt to deplete the resources of a computer or a network of computers by sending large amounts of traffic to them, making them unusable for user needs [34]. The basic principle of DDoS attacks is to exploit a large number of zombie sources spread across multiple sites to target a victim. The attacker is primarily interested in two things: bandwidth exhaustion and resource depletion [35]. This would have a negative impact on the performance and reputation of the server, which makes these attacks extremely important. The authority and performance of the server would be compromised, hence the importance of detecting such attacks [36].

There are various types of DDoS attacks which can be classified into three categories as illustrated in Fig. 3.

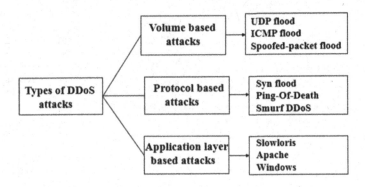

Fig. 3. Types of DDoS attacks

Volume based attacks: ICMP floods, UDP floods, and other faked packet attacks are examples of these types of attacks. The attacker's primary purpose is to use the bandwidth of the victim's website.

Protocol based attacks: SYN floods, fragmented packet attacks, Ping of Death, Smurf attacks, and others are among them. The attacker's primary purpose is to consume server resources.

Application layer based attacks: Attacks such as the Zero-day attack, Slowloris, and others fall under this category. The attacker's main purpose is to exploit weaknesses in application layer services.

5.3   Machine Learning Based Methods

In recent years, Machine Learning (ML) approaches have been widely employed to detect threats in SDN environments. The basic idea of Machine Learning is to automatically learn from a set of data in order to recognize patterns. Machine learning techniques are divided into three categories: supervised, unsupervised, and semi-supervised [37]. We present in Fig. 4 the various Machine Learning (ML) methods used for DDoS detection in SDN environment.

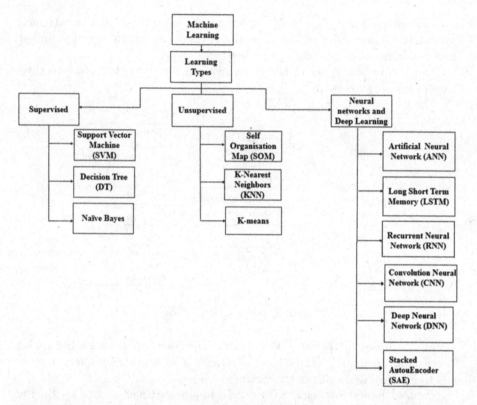

Fig. 4. Overview of Machine Learning approaches used for DDoS threats detection

The following section details the existing studies using Machine Learning techniques to detect DDoS in SDN.

5.3.1 Support Vector Machine (SVM)

The Support Vector Machine (SVM) was first presented by Vapnik [38] and has received considerable attention in the machine learning research community. It uses the supervised learning method to do classification and regression. An SVM algorithm generates a model based on a collection of trained examples, each of which is marked as a method separated into two classes, and predicts that the new example will fall into one of the two. The classic SVM works well for classification, and several studies have incorporated numerous improved methods based on the SVM.

Li et al. [39] suggested a model for DDoS detection using the SVM algorithm. The proposed method used packet-in messages to acquire traffic data and extract the value of some essential features, such as the source IP address, using a ML framework. The distribution of these features is then measured using entropy. Through training the model with normal and abnormal traffic data and according to the experimental tests, the proposed approach can identify DDoS threats with a high degree of efficiency. Moreover, the authors used a small number of features, which is insufficient to cover all attack behaviors. The features in the training module are only extracted from the packet header without further evaluation of the payload. Therefore, the attacker can easily embed malicious code in the payload packets to fool the detection systems. As a result, their accuracy in detecting application-level threats is low. The authors in [40], presented a hybrid method that merges two machine learning methods: Support Vector Machine (SVM) and Self Organizing Maps (SOM) [41] to protect the network from DDoS threats. The SVM is employed for the detection of DDoS threats that it has learned from the dataset, while the SOM model can be used to identify new types of threats. The evaluation results showed that the hybrid machine learning models outperformed the simple machine learning models in terms of accuracy and detection rate. However, the presented detection approach needs to be tested with recent real-world traffic datasets. In [42], the authors employed different ML methods to detect DDoS in Software Defined Network (SDN). The performance of several machine learning methods in a classification problem is evaluated. The authors used a dataset, which is a set of TCP traffic between certain sites derived from experimental results. The detection and prevention are carried out with the help of the controller. It maintains an access control list (ACL) that divides the TCP traffic into two types: normal and malicious. The labelled traffic set is then employed by machine learning algorithms, and the SVM method has been found to outperform other machine learning algorithms. However, the authors used only the TCP flood attack and a unique topology. We can note that the hybrid model has higher accuracy, a lower false alarm rate, and a higher detection rate compared to a simple SVM machine learning model.

5.3.2   Naive Bayes

It's a classification method based on Bayes' Theorem [43]. It predicts the probabilities of membership in each class, like the probability that a given record or data point belongs to a particular class. The class with the highest probability is considered the most likely class [44]. The author in [45] presented a system for DDoS mitigation using machine learning in a multi-SDN controller context. The Naive Bayes classifier is used to recognize the flow features extracted by the SDN controller. When malicious behavior is detected, the SDN controller in the attacker's network receives an automatic alert and a deny IP flow is created. The proposed method gives a high accuracy, with a value of 98%. However, it requires extensive implementation. In [46], the authors employed various Machine Learning approaches, such as Naive Bayes, which gave the highest detection rate for DDoS detection in the SDN controller. The presented method contains two modules, namely signature Intrusion Detection System (IDS) and advanced IDS. The Signature IDS module used ML methods like k-NN, Naive Bayes, k-means [47], and k-medoids [48] to classify traffic flows as normal or abnormal and locate a group of hosts with abnormal behaviour. The Advanced IDS module then checks packets sent by these hosts with abnormal characteristics to determine whether they are abnormal or authorized users. Since only hosts with abnormal behavior need to be evaluated, the processing time of the Advanced IDS module is reduced. We can notice that the Naive Bayes approach can successfully detect DDoS. Does the combination of the Naive Bayes method with another method give better accuracy rates and better results?

5.3.3   Decision Tree (DT)

The Decision Tree is one of the most fundamental approaches used in machine learning and data mining. In decision data analysis, a decision tree can be used to visually and clearly show the decision making [49]. In this method, the data set is examined and created. As a result, if a new data element is presented for classification, the previous dataset will classify it accurately. The DDoS threats are detected using the DT technique.

Sudar et al. [50] developed a Machine Learning (ML) method called Decision Tree (DT) and Support Vector Machine (SVM) for DDoS threat detection in SDN. The authors detected and selected essential characteristics for further detection. The dataset is then transmitted through the SVM classifier and DT module in the next phase. Based on the flag value, classifiers divide the traffic dataset into two categories: attack and normal (0 or 1). Otherwise, the controller will determine the typical traffic packets' routing path. When a DDoS issue is recognized using the SVM classifier and DT, the controller will transmit the forwarding table to process the payload. The experiments showed that SVM outperforms Decision tree in the simulated setting. In addition, the authors used multiple controllers to solve the single point of failure problem. Moreover, the authors did not specify how they used the multiple controllers and how they implemented the proposed method to detect DDoS. In [51], the authors developed a DEcision Tree Pro(DETPro) system for DDoS detection and mitigation in SDN. MODET, a modified decision tree technique, is used by DETPro to quickly detect DDoS. Initially, the POX controller collects data using the OpenFlow (OF) protocol and sFlow-RT [52]. They employed information gain after data collection to choose significant network properties from the data. Finally, they developed the decision tree model with Gini impurity [53] and used the Pessimistic Error Pruning (PEP) [54] approach to decrease the running time and increase generalization ability. They offered a dynamic white list approach in the DDoS threat mitigation module that may recognize benign traffic. When the network is subject to DDoS threats, the mitigation module helps the POX controller apply additional flow rules to ensure that legitimate users can communicate. According to experimental results, DETPro is able to detect DDoS threats at an early stage and successfully protect the network. Besides, the proposed method has high accuracy and a high detection rate. Tonkal et al. [55] presented a method to classify SDN traffic as normal or threat traffic using a machine learning method equipped with Neighbourhood Component Analysis (NCA) [56]. They used a public DDoS attack SDN Dataset involving 23 features. They effectuated a preprocessing step to extract the most important features using the NCA algorithm. Then they classified the obtained dataset using different ML algorithms. They found that the DT method worked well compared to other considered algorithms, with 100% classification achievement. Preamthaisong et al. [57] suggested a technique based on the combination of DT and a genetic algorithm, namely GA-DT to detect DDoS threats in SDN. Initially, the GA wrapper model was used to compress the data dimensions by selecting the most important attributes to examine during the intrusion detection procedure. The data was then classified as normal or DDoS using the extracted features and a DT algorithm. The performance of the GA-DT method was compared to various other machine learning classifiers. According to the results, the suggested approach surpasses existing classifiers in terms of the accuracy of intrusion.

We can note that the modified Decision Tree method gives better results than the simple DT method, but it is more complex and more expensive.

5.3.4   K-Nearest Neighbors (KNN)

KNN is a supervised learning approach that can be used to solve a variety of problems, including security problems [58]. The K-nearest neighbor algorithm is based on the clustering of items with similar features; it computes the class type of a test example according to its k nearest neighbors. The value of k in the KNN depends on the size of the dataset and the type of classification task. If $k = 1$, the case is simply assigned to the nearest neighbor class. Larger values of k can make the classification results more reliable, but they also make the class boundaries less apparent [59].

In [60], the authors presented a DDoS detection approach based on ML technique in SDN environment. There are two approaches to implementing the proposed strategy. First, DDoS threats are detected based on the degree of attacks. Second, classifications will be performed using the ML method. The authors employed an updated KNN algorithm to find DDoS patterns based on four parameters: flow length, flow duration, flow size, and flow ratio. According to the testing results, the presented technique can successfully identify DDoS. Xu et al. [61] also proposed two novel approaches for DDoS detection in SDN: Kmeans++ and Fast K-Nearest Neighbors (K-FKNN) to improve classical KNN. The training data is preprocessed using the K-means++ method. This information is then used in DDoS detection software. The K-FKNN initializer, K-FKNN-based detector, and DDoS Mitigation are all part of the application plane. The K-FKNN Initializer is employed to initialize the values of the K-FKNN algorithm's parameters. The control plane sends vector data to the K-FKNN detector. It preprocesses the data to detect DDoS threats by normalizing the feature data in this vector using the K-FKNN algorithm. If the traffic is identified as a DDoS threat, the controller is notified, and the action record in the flow table is removed. The controller sends this flow entry to the switch, which drops the network's harmful flow to safeguard the network. The results of the experiments showed that the presented method is effective and that its detection is rather stable. Nam et al. [62] presented a technique for DDoS threat detection using Seft-Organizing-Map (SOM) and K-Nearest-Neighbor (KNN). The authors used the first SOM in order to reduce dimensionality. Then, they presented two classification methods. In the first one, they combined SOM and KNN. In the second method, they used SOM with center-distributed classification, where SOM is exclusively trained on normal traffic samples in this case. The distance between each input sample and a universal reference point is then calculated by the algorithm, where the trained data is centered around this point with a predetermined threshold. If the distance is less than that threshold, it is considered normal; otherwise, it is considered abnormal. The experimental results showed that the first approach, which merged SOM and KNN, performed better than the second method relating to detection rate and false positive rate.

The presented methods use the modified KNN method and KNN merged with another method for DDoS detection in SDN. The different methods are effective, with a good detection rate and a low false positive rate. However, the presented methods are time-consuming and complex.

5.4   Deep Learning Based Methods

Deep learning is a type of machine learning that has a significant impact on computing and data processing by employing many layers of non-linear processing to extract meaningful features from direct input [63]. This data can be text, images, or network traffic. Deep learning is now widely regarded as the most effective method for developing highly accurate data classification models. Input layers, hidden layers, and output layers are the three levels in a deep neural network. Deep learning algorithms have gained much more popularity for intrusion detection. In [6], the authors presented a load balancing technique that uses network and application information to balance the load of SDN across multiple sensors. The presented model may balance the batch of applications between sensors connected via SDN. The authors evaluated the proposed method using a variety of datasets such as NSL-KDD. Then, they compare the results of their model with those of well-known heuristic-based models. Furthermore, they classified intrusion attacks using an entropy-based active learning approach. In terms of sparse and dense datasets, the created model can identify patterns with high accuracy.

In this section, we provide an overview of Deep learning algorithms such as Artificial Neural Network (ANN), Stacked Autoencoder (SAE), Deep Neural Network (DNN), Convolutional Neural Network (CNN) and Recurrent Neural Network (RNN). Then, we present research studies using these methods to detect DDoS in the SDN environment.

5.4.1   Artificial Neural Network (ANN)

ANN is a sort of artificial intelligence that imitates some mental capabilities. It has a natural tendency to remember what it has learned from previous experiences. An ANN consists of a sequence of layers. Weighted connections connect all neurons in each layer to all neurons in the preceding and following layers [64]. It employs a non-parametric strategy. The network structure and amount of inputs have an impact on performance and accuracy.

Hannache et al. [65] proposed a Neural Network based Traffic Flow Classifier (TFC-NN) to detect DDoS in SDN in real time. The authors began by creating a dataset to train the TFC-NN. The dataset contains examples of regular traffic as well as malicious traffic related to well-known DDoS threats that took advantage of SDN's high-level programmability and monitoring capabilities. After that, a TFC-NN (Traffic Flow Classifier based Neural Network) is presented. TFC-NN is trained and deployed using a real SDN architecture. Finally, a mitigation technique integrating TFCNN live classification is shown. The TFC-NN classified the data with a global accuracy of 96.13%. In [66], the authors developed a DDoS detection system using entropy and neural network in SDN. The suggested technique employs an entropy approach on the switch to distinguish between normal and abnormal traffic. The anomaly detection module gathers the flow table and extracts the necessary information for categorization when abnormal traffic occur. With the use of a PSO-BP neural network, the attack detection module assesses whether a client is normal or malicious. The experimental results showed that the suggested solution improves detection accuracy, and increases detection speed.

In the presented methods, the ANN method is merged with another approach to detect DDoS, which makes the proposed method more complex. Is using the simple ANN method sufficient to detect DDoS attacks?

5.4.2 Stacked Autoencoder (SAE)

Stacked Autoencoder (SAE) is a Deep Learning (DL) method that uses stacked sparse autoencoders and a softmax classifier to learn and classify unsupervised features. It consists of numerous layers of sparse autoencoders, with each hidden layer's output coupled to the input of the next hidden layer. A stacked autoencoder's basic structure is as follows [67]: the autoencoder is trained and learned data is obtained using the input data; the learned data from the previous layer is utilized as input for the next layer, and so on until training is completed. The cost function is reduced using the back propagation technique once all of the hidden layers have been trained, and weights are updated with the training data to achieve fine tuning.

Niyar et al. [68] developed an SDN-based DDoS detection system which includes a Stacked Autoencoder (SAE) based DL method. This system is categorized as a network application that runs on the controller. It begins by extracting 68 flow features from the collected network data. Then, to reduce features and detect DDoS threats, a deep learning model is used. The performance of the suggested system is measured using a data set that includes both normal Internet traffic and various DDoS threats. In [69], the authors presented a Deep Learning model based on Stacked Auto Encoders (SAE) to identify a DDoS threat in SDN. This suggested system was created specifically for IoT traffic flows. First, the authors introduced sFlow and adaptive polling based sampling on the data layer to reduce switch processing and network overhead. Second, in the control plane, they used Snort IDS in conjunction with the Stacked Autoencoders (SAE) deep learning model to improve detection accuracy. The results showed that when sFlow is used instead of adaptive pooling, the detection rate of the model is higher. The authors in [70] presented a novel Deep Learning framework to identify DDoS threats in SDN based VANETs using Stacked Sparse Autoencoder (SSAE) and Softmax classifier. SSAE was used to reduce the dimensionality of the dataset received from the SDN-based VANET, and the most significant characteristics were extracted. These characteristics were then fed into the Softmax classifier as input. The experimental results proved that the proposed deep method to detect DDoS threats performed well compared to machine learning classifiers and previous studies. In [71], the authors detected DDoS in Software Defined Networking (SDN) using various Deep Learning algorithms such as Stacked Auto-Encoder Multilayer Perceptron (SAE-MLP). The proposed method consists of three steps. The first step is data preprocessing which involves removing redundant inputs from the dataset by identifying the type of the variables. In the second step, the authors applied multiple Deep Learning algorithms to classify the traffic into normal and malicious classes based on the features provided in the dataset. Finally, they evaluated the used models using different metrics. The experimental results showed that the Stacked Auto-Encoder Multilayer Perceptron (SAE-MLP) gives the highest accuracy with a value of 99.75%.

5.4.3 Deep Neural Network (DNN)

The DNN is known as a multilayer perceptron due to its many hidden layers. The DNN can assist in feature extraction and representation learning tasks due to this multi-layer feature, which allows complex functions to be stated with fewer parameters [72]. In DNN, layers are classified into three types. In general, we consider the first layer as the input layer, the last layer as the output layer, and the intermediate layers as hidden layers.

Makuvaza et al. [73] presented a Deep Neural Network (DNN) method for real time DDoS threat detection in SDN. First, the authors extracted the best features from the CICIDS 2017 dataset. They divided the data into training and testing sets. The model was then trained and tested. Thus, it can decide whether the traffic is a benign attack or DDoS traffic. The experimental results showed that the presented control plane Deep Learning model detects correctly DDoS threats with a high accuracy, with a value of 97.59% using fewer resources and less time. In [30], the authors proposed a two-level security detection system for DDoS threats. In the first level, an open source intrusion detection system named Snort is used to identify the DDoS threat signature. At the second level, the proposed technique used two ML methods, DNN and SVM, to predict DDoS attacks. The KDD Cup 1999 dataset was used to train and evaluate machine learning methods for DDoS classification. According to the experimental results, the DNN provided greater accuracy compared to the SVM.

Deep Neural Network gives good results in the detection of DDoS because of its ability to represent features at multiple levels. However, the more complex the neural network, the longer it takes to train the model. In other words, the deeper the neural network, the more complex it is.

5.4.4   Convolutional Neural Network (CNN)

CNN is a representative and well-known deep learning method that combines convolution processing and depth structure. CNN, in particular, uses a multi layer perceptual variant design that requires minimal preprocessing. The input and output layers, along with many hidden layers such as convolution, pooling, and the full connection layer, form the basic framework of CNN [74]. CNN uses less preprocessing than other classification algorithms and does not depend on feature design, including prior knowledge, which are two of its main advantages. Convolutional neural networks have enabled significant advances in the field of network security.

Nurghana et al. [75] presented a Deep Learning framework to detect slow DDoS threats in the SDN environment. The proposed model used the REST API of the SDN controller to collect statistics on traffic flows from SDN switches and analyze them to detect a slow DDoS threat. The DDoS detection module is built around a Convolutional Neural Network-Long Short Term Memory (CNN-LSTM) model. The authors started by creating their own dataset that includes benign and slow DDoS traffic flows. They then trained, validated, and tested their model using their dataset. In addition, the authors performed several tests using a synthetically created traffic flow dataset to evaluate the detection performance of their hybrid CNN-LSTM model after identifying the best set of hyper parameter values. The experimental results showed that the proposed model is highly accurate and outperforms various deep learning models like Multilayer Perceptron (MLP) and 1-Class Support Vector Machine (1-Class SVM). However, the presented method is time consuming and not affordable for real-time detection. In [76], the authors suggested a framework to detect DDoS using Deep Learning in the context of an SDN. In order to detect Flow-based the suggested model employs CNN. The SDN controller has been programmed with a system architecture for the deep CNN ensemble. Flow-based attributes and features for the SDN were derived from the CICIDS2017 dataset. According to the performance results, the proposed framework is effective against DDoS threats on the SDN controller. The authors did not compare the proposed method with other comparable studies, although they provided a comparison of several reference datasets.

We can note that the convolutional neural network (CNN) has the ability to properly detect DDoS attack traffic in the SDN environment.

5.4.5   Recurrent Neural Network (RNN)

An RNN is a feed forward neural network that has been extended to recognize patterns in a data set. RNNs are called recurrent because they perform the same task for each element in a sequence, with the result depending on previous computations [77]. The sequential information is stored in the hidden state of the recurrent network, which can span multiple time steps as it cascades forward to perform processing for each new input.

In [78], the authors developed a DDoS detection system in SDN environment using Recurrent Neural Network (RNN) with an autoencoder. At the input layer, they merged RNN-autoencoder with softmax regression model to classify the network traffic into malicious or normal. They evaluated the proposed model with the newly released dataset CICDDoS2019, which includes a wide range of DDoS threats and fills in the gaps in existing datasets. The authors compared their models with other techniques such as SVM. The experimental results showed that proposed DDoSNet outperforms the other techniques with an accuracy of 99%. But, the presented approach requires huge amount of resources. Li et al. [79] proposed a DDoS detection and defense framework based on various Deep Learning methods such as Recurrent Neural Network (RNN), Long Short-Term Memory (LSTM), and Convolutional Neural Network (CNN). The presented method is used with OpenFlow switches. The deep learning model is employed for feature reduction and DDoS threat detection once the network traffic feature information is collected and analyzed. After the detection of DDoS threats the authors putted the Deep Learning DDoS defence in place. The results of a real-time DDoS threat experiment showed that the defense approach obtained an accuracy rate of 98%. Moreover, using the proposed method, the synchronized work of controllers may be disrupted and the network performance may be degraded. The authors in [80] presented a real-time DDoS detection approach for an SDN controller using BiLSTM-RNN neural network technique. They first used entropy in order to determine the abnormality in the network traffic. After that, a warning signal is triggered, and key features are extracted. The presented system includes four modules: the anomaly detection module, the flow table collection module, the feature extraction module, and the attack detection module. The results revealed that the suggested system can efficiently identify DDoS threats while also reducing the overhead on the SDN controller. However, the authors must use a recent dataset to evaluate the proposed method. Besides, this method is only applicable to specific types of DDoS threats.

The recurrent neural network (RNN) is the most widely used technique for classifying and analyzing data sequences. It's also a potent strategy that can improve the pace of DDoS detection in an SDN environment and exhibit outstanding results in sequence learning.

5.5   Discussion

In this section, we present an overview of the presented methods used for DDoS detection in SDN. We classify them into two categories: Machine Learning (ML) and Deep Learning (DL) methods. We also present the different types of DDoS detected threats with the advantages and drawbacks of each method. We summarize in Table 3 and Table 4 the ML and DL methods respectively.

Table 3. Summary of Machine Learning methods used for DDoS threat detection

Ref/Years	Algorithms	Datasets	Types of DDoS	Accuracy	Advantages	Limitations
[50] (2021)	SVM DT	KDD Cup 99	UDP flood ICMP flood SYN flood fragmented packet ping of death smurf DDoS GET\POST floods	85%	Multiple controllers are used	Recent dataset must be used Low precision
[60] (2020)	KNN	NSLKDD	TCP flood UDP flood ICMP flood	98%	High accuracy High precision	Time consuming The simulated network topology is small
[51] (2019)	Modified DT	Their dataset	SYN flood HTTP POST attack HTTP GET attack	97%	High performance High detection rate	Expensive cost Detects and mitigates specific types of DDoS threats
[57] (2019)	GA-DT	Their dataset	TCP SYN flood UDP flooding ICMP flooding TCP Kill	99%	High accuracy Recent types of DDoS threats are used	Real testbed must be included Consumes a lot of time
[61] (2019)	FKNN K means ++	NSL-KDD	ICMP flood UDP flood TCP flood	98%	High accuracy Easy to implement	Time consuming Puts a lot of strain on the SDN's resources
[62] (2018)	SOM-KNN	DDoS Attack 2007	ICMP flood UDP flood SYN flood	98%	Detects various types of DDoS threats Lowering the computational overhead	High processing time High false positive rate It should be improved in terms of detecting precision
[39] (2018)	SVM	DARPA1999 Their dataset	TCP flood ICMP flood UDP flood	98%	Entropy application minimizes the amount of calculations	The dataset is small The number of extracted features is negligible
[40] (2018)	SVM-SOM	Their dataset	TCP flood ICMP flood UDP flood	98%	High accuracy High detection rate Low false positive rate	Recent real-time traffic data sets should be used
[30] (2018)	SVM	KDD Cup 99	TCP flood	92%	Used Real-time data sets	Recent dataset must be used No distributed environment is used
[45] (2018)	Naive-Bayes	NSLKDD	SYN flooding	98%	Used a 41 feature DDOS dataset High precision The data set cannot reflect the current trend in network attacks	Requires extensive and enforceable implementation Training and testing split ratio not mentioned Additional calculation time is required
[42] (2017)	SVM	Their dataset	TCP flood	80%	Used real time dataset	Used only TCP flood Unique topology is used
[46] (2016)	Naive bayes KNN K-means K-medois	Their dataset	TCP flood	94%	High detection rate Various ML algorithms are used	Only the DDoS threats are considered Difficulty handling large amount of data

Table 3 shows that various ML techniques are used to detect DDoS threats in the SDN environment. We can distinguish several types of DDoS threats such as flooding attacks (UDP flood, ICMP flood, TCP SYN flood) and application layer attacks (HTTP flood, SMTP flood) [81]. These types of DDoS threats are detected using the different ML methods. Besides, public datasets are used such as NSLKDD [45,60,61], KDD Cup 99 [50], DARPA1999 [39], and DDoS Attack 2007 [62]. However, these datasets are not specific to the SDN environment and are not updated. In addition, some of these datasets have several drawbacks, such as the DDoS attack 2007 [62] dataset, which is collected from different locations, at different times, and in different situations, making it impossible to describe a consistent traffic pattern. Most of the observations in the KDD CUP'99 dataset are highly redundant, and therefore similar observations occur in both the training and testing sets. We can also note that the ML algorithms can correctly identify DDoS threats. In order to improve the efficiency of ML approaches, we present the accuracy rate given by these methods, which represents the number

Table 4. Summary of Deep Learning methods used for DDoS threat detection

Ref/Years	Algorithms	Datasets	Types of DDoS	Accuracy	Advantages	Limitations
[73] (2021)	DNN	CICIDS 2017	DDoS attacks	96,6%	Real time detection Lower time High accuracy	Limited number of features
[70] (2021)	SSAE	Their dataset	TCP flooding UDP flooding ICMP flooding	96,9%	High accuracy Low training time model Works with limited memory	Computational complexity Expensive cost
[75] (2020)	CNN-LSTM	Their dataset	UDP flows HTTP flows	99,9%	High accuracy Used with large dataset	Time consuming Is not affordable for real-time
[69] (2020)	SAE	Their dataset	HTTP flood DNS flood ICMP flood UDP flood Smurf flood IP flood	91%	High accuracy Low false positive rate	Failed to distinguish between DDoS threats and Flash events
[78] (2020)	RNN	CICDDoS2019	SYN flooding UDP-Lag UDP flood	99%	High accuracy	Requires huge amount of resources Each type of attack is not classified separately
[76] (2020)	CNN	CICIDS2017	DDoS attacks	99,4%	Detection is more accurate Real time detection	Spatial resolution is reduced Prevention method is not available
[65] (2020)	NN	Their dataset	TCP SYN flood ICMP PoD UDP flood	96%	Fast method Real time detection	Limited to the detection of specific types of DDoS threats A small dataset is used
[66] (2019)	PSO-BP NN	Their dataset	ICMP flood UDP flood TCP SYN flood	97%	Fast detection speed Reduces the overhead of the SDN controller	The model is trained offline A huge number of labeled training datasets is required
[80] (2019)	BiLSTM-RNN	Their dataset	UDP flood	98%	Real time detection Reduces SDN controller overhead	Recent dataset must be used Is only applicable to specific types of DDoS threats
[79] (2018)	CNN-RNN-LSTM	ISCX 2012	UDP flood SYN flood ARP flood Smurf attack PingofDeath attack	98%	Dependence on hardware and software is reduced Easy to adapt the changes in real-time High accuracy	Processing overhead Synchronized work of controllers may be disrupted Network performance may be degraded
[68] (2016)	SAE-NN	Their dataset	ICMP attacks UDP attacks TCP attacks	95%	High accuracy Low false positives	The performance of the controller in large networks is limited Important processing overhead per packet for feature extraction increases bur- den of the controller A large amount of DDoS traffic is required

of accurately anticipated observations divided by the total number of observations. They give high accuracy, with a value above 90% for most methods. We can also see that different approaches give high precision, which is the ratio of accurately predicted positive observations to total expected positive observations. As we can see, three papers used the same dataset (NSLKDD): [45, 60, 61], we can compare these methods. The different methods give very high accuracy, with a value of 98%. We can note that we cannot choose the ML method based on the accuracy metric. We can consider the advantages and limitations of each method in our choice.

Table 2 presents also the advantages and limitations of the presented ML methods. These methods successfully detect DDoS threats with a higher detection rate and a lower risk of false alarms. Furthermore, by detecting DDoS threats, they reduce their impact and improve the accuracy of the security solution. However, ML approaches have drawbacks, such as high costs and long processing times.

As shown in Table 3, the Deep Learning methods are used for detecting several types of DDoS in the SDN environment. Besides, it is seen that several datasets were employed to detect threat traffic. Public datasets were used by some of the researchers, such as CICIDS2017 [73,76], CICDDoS2019 [78], and ISCX2012 [79] which contained network traffic data from traditional network typologies. These datasets are useful for assessing the performance of DL techniques employed in threat traffic detection. However, because the SDN design differs from traditional network architecture, it has its own set of attack vectors in addition to the current ones. Besides, the increasing volume and variety of threats necessitates the use of up-to-date data sets. As a result, researchers employ datasets gathered through the SDN architecture in their studies [68,69,75,80]. The different datasets were built with the SDN architecture and included the most recent SDN DDoS traffic data. We can also notice that the presented DL techniques give high accuracy, with a value higher than 95%. They can successfully detect DDoS threats. We can see that two papers used the CICIDS2017 dataset [73,76]. The CNN method outperforms the DNN method in terms of accuracy, with a value of 99,4%. In addition, Deep Learning methods have several advantages. Most of the methods are used for real-time detection and have a low false positive rate. Besides, they reduce the training time model and work with limited memory. However, these methods have drawbacks, such as high computation, as these approaches require enough traffic statistics obtained from different SDN layers to perform effective learning. Besides, these methods have such high training costs as they require a large amount of data and iterations to converge.

In comparison with Machine Learning approaches, Deep Learning methods are more suitable for processing massive high-dimensional training datasets because of their ability to learn features and extract hierarchical features. However, the more complex the neural network is, the longer it takes to train the model. Furthermore, increasing the volume of training datasets improves the performance of the deep learning model while also increasing the training time and complexity. As a result, there is a compromise between the model's detection performance and its complexity.

6   Open Issues and Challenges

In order to provide efficient ML and DL approaches to detect DDoS in SDN environment some open issues and challenges need to addressed. In this section, we present the challenges and future research directions. In what follows, we first present the challenges associated with the SDN environment.

Network scalability: In SDN, network scalability is a major concern. When a single controller is installed on the control plane, as the size of the network and number of flows increase, the controller typically has scalability issues due to its computational limitations [1]. To address the scalability problem, distributed multi-controller platforms must be used. A distributed multi controller platform is made up of numerous local controllers and a logically centralized root controller. The root controller has full access to all switches and has a global view of the entire network.

Network reliability: Reliability is critical in any software development project [82]. If a system fails, users should be notified, and the remedy should work automatically. Software reliability refers to the likelihood that it will perform as expected in a given environment and for a certain period of time. The network management setup of the SDN controller must be intelligent and validated in order to boost network availability and prevent and handle problems. Reliability is considered a major issue in SDN due to the single point failure of the controller [83]. If just one central controller is in charge of the entire network, and if the central network fails, the entire network may cease to function or collapse. To solve this problem, a cluster of controllers can be used to control and administer an SDN network. When a request to update a flow table is made, it may well be processed by a group of controllers. Besides, to improve network reliability, software providers and developers should focus on utilizing the major controller functionalities.

Network security: The network security of SDN is another issue. The decoupling of the data plane and control plane decreases the complexity of network devices and gives flexible network management [1]. Since the switches in the data plane have no understanding, they simply send raw packets of information to the controller. Unfortunately, this behavior presents a real weakness that attackers can exploit by flooding the controller with a large number of flow requests. Besides, DDoS attacks on OpenFlow switches can be launched using a variety of network devices [84]. Attackers can use hijacked switches to stifle legitimate traffic flows or slow down the network. By providing fake traffic packets to the controller for rule making, these hijacked switches can also overwhelm the controller. Therefore, these switches can create a bottleneck in the network. Therefore, the research community faces a significant challenge in protecting switches from compromise. In addition, security of the communication channels between switches and controllers requires more work to establish and implement. If these communication lines are breached the network performance could be harmed. Switches in SDN-based networks rely on controllers for each inflow of traffic forwarding rules. Therefore, for each mismatched entry, the switch requests that the controller amend or create a new forwarding rule. As a result, these communication channels are critical in achieving the appropriate degree of performance. A more powerful authentication system is required to guard against man-in-the-middle attacks. The SDN community also has another significant difficulty in the security of these links. An SDN framework must be established to manage and develop solutions for software integrity, remote access management, network threat detection and mitigation, and user authentication and authorization.

Implementing an effective and practical defense system using ML and DL methods also poses some challenges.

In what follows, we present the most important challenges associated with ML and DL approaches.

High quality datasets: Because finding an appropriate dataset for a given sort of DDoS threat is challenging, most researchers rely on existing datasets or construct their own. The main disadvantage of using an existing dataset is that it is quite old and therefore unsuitable for assessing the robustness of a system [85]. Besides, it is well known that threats like DDoS adapt to advanced strategies and become more complex in order to evade any security measures, which means that relying on conclusions based on old datasets is not a wise practice. Even if researchers use a synthetic dataset, it is difficult to simulate a real-world dataset, i.e., one that reflects attacks that have actually occurred and caused damage to a victim. Another concern with the dataset is privacy, as companies that have previously been subjected to DDoS threats are reluctant to share important data and log files with the general public.

Features selection: It a technique for selecting a subset of relevant features from a large number of options. Removing extraneous data increases learning accuracy, decreases computation time, and makes the learning model or data easier to grasp [86]. In practice, not all of the variables in a dataset are valuable when building a machine learning model. The addition of redundant variables reduces the model's generalization competence and may also reduce a classifier's overall precision. Furthermore, adding more variables to a model leads to the development of a complicated model. The selection of important features is an important issue because ML and DL approaches are used to train and verify the selected features so that they can effectively predict attacks. Another problem facing researchers is determining a strategy that selects the optimal features from among the many other features.

Security of ML and DL methods: The security is another issue for ML and DL methods. These methods are vulnerable to various security threats, which can be divided into two categories depending on the training state of the learning model. Threats before or during model training and threats after model training are the two categories. For example, the training set poisoning attack is the malicious modification of a training set in order to deceive the prediction of a machine learning model [87]. According to studies, a small percentage of well designed poisoned training data can cause a huge drop in the machine learning model's performance. Besides, the attackers try always to generate new attacks. In this situation, using verifiable information to prepare ML and DL models may not be a successful strategy to distinguish threats because of the emergence of new threats.

Training time: This is also a major problem for ML and DL methods. Model training is very time consuming, especially for deep learning methods. Most of these methods can take several hours, which can be a waste of time and require additional computation. In addition, the large amount of time required to train the models can affect the performance of the proposed methods. Even if they give good accuracy and results, the training time does not allow the method to be chosen.

7 Conclusion

This article provided a survey of Machine Learning methods used for DDoS detection in SDN environment. First, we present the properties and architecture of SDN. Then, we enumerate the different threats against the SDN environment based on which part of the SDN paradigm they target and which security aspects are affected, such as availability, integrity, and confidentiality. We also review the main recent works using Machine Learning and Deep Learning approaches to detect DDoS threats and discuss their strengths and weaknesses. We compare them on the basis of the accuracy rate. We also discussed key challenges and future research goals for Machine Learning and Deep Learning methods in the SDN environment, such as high-quality training datasets and a distributed multi-controller platform. More efforts need to be made to provide an effective DDoS detection method in the SDN environment (see open issues and challenges Sect. 6).

References

1. Kreutz, D., Ramos, F.M.V., Esteves Verissimo, P., Esteve Rothenberg, C., Azodol-molky, S., Uhlig, S.: Software-defined networking: a comprehensive survey. Proc. IEEE **103**(1), 14–76 (2015)
2. Masoudi, R., Ghaffari, A.: Software defined networks: a survey. J. Netw. Comput. Appl. **67**, 1–25 (2016)
3. Krishnan, P., Najeem, J.S.: A review of security, threats and mitigation approaches for SDN architecture. Int. J. Innov. Technol. Exp. Eng. **8**, 389–393 (2019)
4. Lew, J., et al.: Analyzing machine learning workloads using a detailed GPU simu-lator. In: 2019 IEEE International Symposium on Performance Analysis of Systems and Software (ISPASS), pp. 151–152. IEEE (2019)
5. Khashab, F., Moubarak, J., Feghali, A., Bassil, C.: DDoS attack detection and mitigation in SDN using machine learning. In: 2021 IEEE 7th International Con-ference on Network Softwarization (NetSoft), pp. 395–401. IEEE (2021)
6. Ahmed, U., Lin, J.C.-W., Srivastava, G.: Network-aware SDN load balancer with deep active learning based intrusion detection model. In: 2021 International Joint Conference on Neural Networks (IJCNN), pp. 1–6. IEEE (2021)
7. Ahmad, Z., Khan, A.S., Shiang, C.W., Abdullah, J., Ahmad, F.: Network intru-sion detection system: a systematic study of machine learning and deep learning approaches. Trans. Emerg. Telecommun. Technol. **32**(1), e4150 (2021)
8. Xie, J., et al.: A survey of machine learning techniques applied to software defined networking (SDN): research issues and challenges. IEEE Commun. Surv. Tut. **21**(1), 393–430 (2018)
9. Gupta, S., Grover, D.: A comprehensive review on detection of DDoS attacks using ML in SDN environment. In: 2021 International Conference on Artificial Intelligence and Smart Systems (ICAIS), pp. 1158–1163. IEEE (2021)
10. Aljuhani, A.: Machine learning approaches for combating distributed denial of service attacks in modern networking environments. IEEE Access **9**, 42236–42264 (2021)
11. Nadeau, T.D., Gray, K.: SDN: Software Defined Networks (2013)

12. Nadeau, T., Pan, P.: Software driven networks problem statement. Network Working Group Internet-Draft, 30 September 2011
13. Latah, M., Toker, L.: Artificial intelligence enabled software-defined networking: a comprehensive overview. IET Netw. **8**(2), 79–99 (2019)
14. Nunes, B.A.A., Mendonca, M., Nguyen, X.-N., Obraczka, K., Turletti, T.: A survey of software-defined networking: past, present, and future of programmable networks. IEEE Commun. Surv. Tut. **16**(3), 1617–1634 (2014)
15. Xu, L., Huang, J., Hong, S., Zhang, J., Gu, G.: Attacking the brain: races in the {SDN} control plane. In: 26th {USENIX} Security Symposium, {USENIX} Security 2017, pp. 451–468 (2017)
16. Bernardo, D.V.: Software-defined networking and network function virtualization security architecture. Internet Engineering Task Force, Fremont, CA, USA (2014). https://tools.ietf.org/html/draftbernardo-sec-arch-sdnnvf-architecture-00
17. Yang, M., Li, Y., Jin, D., Zeng, L., Wu, X., Vasilakos, A.V.: Software-defined and virtualized future mobile and wireless networks: a survey. Mob. Netw. Appl. **20**(1), 4–18 (2015). https://doi.org/10.1007/s11036-014-0533-8
18. Yuan, W., Deng, P., Taleb, T., Wan, J., Bi, C.: An unlicensed taxi identification model based on big data analysis. IEEE Trans. Intell. Transp. Syst. **17**(6), 1703–1713 (2015)
19. Jing, Q., Vasilakos, A.V., Wan, J., Lu, J., Qiu, D.: Security of the Internet of Things: perspectives and challenges. Wirel. Netw. **20**(8), 2481–2501 (2014)
20. Namal, S., Ahmad, I., Gurtov, A., Ylianttila, M.: SDN based inter-technology load balancing leveraged by flow admission control. In: 2013 IEEE SDN for Future Networks and Services (SDN4FNS), pp. 1–5. IEEE (2013)
21. Lara, A., Kolasani, A., Ramamurthy, B.: Network innovation using OpenFlow: a survey. IEEE Commun. Surv. Tut. **16**(1), 493–512 (2013)
22. Iqbal, M., Iqbal, F., Mohsin, F., Rizwan, M., Ahmad, F.: Security issues in software defined networking (SDN): risks, challenges and potential solutions. Int. J. Adv. Comput. Sci. Appl. **10**(10), 298–303 (2019)
23. Lotlikar, T., Shah, D.: A survey of potential security threats and counter-measures in SDN: an IoT enabling technology. OSR J. Comput. Eng., 67–74 (2017)
24. Akbaş, M.F., Karaarslan, E., Güngör, C.: A preliminary survey on the security of software-defined networks. Int. J. Appl. Math. Electron. Comput. **4**(Special Issue-1), 184–189 (2016)
25. Mostafa, N., Elazim, A., Sobh, M.A., Bahaa-Eldin, A.M.: Software defined networking: attacks and countermeasures. In: 2018 13th International Conference on Computer Engineering and Systems (ICCES), pp. 555–567. IEEE (2018)
26. Pradhan, A., Mathew, R.: Solutions to vulnerabilities and threats in software defined networking (SDN). Procedia Comput. Sci. **171**, 2581–2589 (2020)
27. Revathi, S., Geetha, A., et al.: A survey of applications and security issues in software defined networking. Int. J. Comput. Netw. Inf. Secur. **9**(3), 21 (2017)
28. Gao, S., Li, Z., Xiao, B., Wei, G.: Security threats in the data plane of software-defined networks. IEEE Netw. **32**(4), 108–113 (2018)
29. Scott-Hayward, S., Natarajan, S., Sezer, S.: A survey of security in software defined networks. IEEE Commun. Surv. Tut. **18**(1), 623–654 (2015)
30. Karan, B.V., Narayan, D.G., Hiremath, P.S.: Detection of DDoS attacks in software defined networks. In: 2018 3rd International Conference on Computational Systems and Information Technology for Sustainable Solutions (CSITSS), pp. 265–270 (2018)

31. Tayfour, O.E., Marsono, M.N.: Collaborative detection and mitigation of distributed denial-of-service attacks on software-defined network. Mob. Netw. Appl. **25**(4), 1338–1347 (2020)
32. Xu, X., Yu, H., Yang, K.: DDoS attack in software defined networks: a survey. ZTE Commun. **15**(3), 13–19 (2017)
33. Lin, B., Zhu, X., Ding, Z.: Research on the vulnerability of software defined network. In: 3rd Workshop on Advanced Research and Technology in Industry, WARTIA 2017, pp. 253–260. Atlantis Press (2017)
34. Mousavi, S.M., St-Hilaire, M.: Early detection of DDoS attacks against SDN controllers. In: 2015 International Conference on Computing, Networking and Communications (ICNC), pp. 77–81. IEEE (2015)
35. Mitrocotsa, A., Douligeris, C.: DDoS attack and defence mechanism: a classification. In: 3rd IEEE International Symposium on Signal Processing and Information Technology, pp. 190–193 (2003)
36. Karoui, K.: Risk analysis linked to network attacks. In: Cyber-Vigilance and Digital Trust: Cyber Security in the Era of Cloud Computing and IoT, pp. 105–140 (2019)
37. Furdek, M., Natalino, C.: Machine learning for optical network security management. In: 2020 Optical Fiber Communications Conference and Exhibition (OFC), pp. 1–3. IEEE (2020)
38. Cortes, C., Vapnik, V.: Support-vector networks. Mach. Learn. **20**(3), 273–297 (1995)
39. Li, D., Yu, C., Zhou, Q., Yu, J.: Using SVM to detect DDoS attack in SDN network. IOP Conf. Ser. Mater. Sci. Eng. **466**, 012003 (2018)
40. Deepa, V., Sudar, K.M., Deepalakshmi, P.: Detection of DDoS attack on SDN control plane using hybrid machine learning techniques. In: 2018 International Conference on Smart Systems and Inventive Technology (ICSSIT), pp. 299–303. IEEE (2018)
41. Van Hulle, M.M.: Self-organizing maps (2012)
42. Meti, N., Narayan, D.G., Baligar, V.P.: Detection of distributed denial of service attacks using machine learning algorithms in software defined networks. In: 2017 International Conference on Advances in Computing, Communications and Informatics (ICACCI), pp. 1366–1371. IEEE (2017)
43. Swinburne, R.: Bayes' theorem. Revue Philosophique de la France Et de l **194**(2) (2004)
44. Webb, G.I., Keogh, E., Miikkulainen, R.: Naïve Bayes. Encycl. Mach. Learn. **15**, 713–714 (2010)
45. Mohammed, S.S., et al.: A new machine learning-based collaborative DDoS mitigation mechanism in software-defined network. In: 2018 14th International Conference on Wireless and Mobile Computing, Networking and Communications (WiMob), pp. 1–8. IEEE (2018)
46. Barki, L., Shidling, A., Meti, N., Narayan, D.G., Mulla, M.M.: Detection of distributed denial of service attacks in software defined networks. In: 2016 International Conference on Advances in Computing, Communications and Informatics (ICACCI), pp. 2576–2581. IEEE (2016)
47. Münz, G., Li, S., Carle, G.: Traffic anomaly detection using k-means clustering. In: GI/ITG Workshop MMBnet, pp. 13–14 (2007)
48. Rustam, Z., Talita, A.S.: Fuzzy kernel k-medoids algorithm for anomaly detection problems. In: AIP Conference Proceedings, vol. 1862, pp. 030154. AIP Publishing LLC. (2017)

49. Arshi, M., Nasreen, M.D., Madhavi, K.: A survey of DDoS attacks using machine learning techniques. In: E3S Web of Conferences, vol. 184, pp. 01052. EDP Sciences (2020)
50. Sudar, K.M., Beulah, M., Deepalakshmi, P., Nagaraj, P., Chinnasamy, P.: Detection of distributed denial of service attacks in SDN using machine learning techniques. In: 2021 International Conference on Computer Communication and Informatics (ICCCI), pp. 1–5. IEEE (2021)
51. Chen, Y., Pei, J., Li, D.: DETPro: a high-efficiency and low-latency system against DDoS attacks in SDN based on decision tree. In: 2019 IEEE International Conference on Communications (ICC), ICC 2019, pp. 1–6. IEEE (2019)
52. Phaal, P.: sFlow version 5 (2004). http://www.sflow.org/sflow_version_5.txt
53. Zhi, T., Luo, H., Liu, Y.: A Gini impurity-based interest flooding attack defence mechanism in NDN. IEEE Commun. Lett. 22(3), 538–541 (2018)
54. Wei, H.: Comparison among methods of decision tree pruning. J. Southwest Jiaotong Univ. (2005)
55. Tonkal, Ö., Polat, H., Başaran, E., Cömert, Z., Kocaoğlu, R.: Machine learning approach equipped with neighbourhood component analysis for DDoS attack detection in software-defined networking. Electronics 10(11), 1227 (2021)
56. Roweis, S., Hinton, G., Salakhutdinov, R.: Neighbourhood component analysis. In: Advances in Neural Information Processes System (NIPS), vol. 17, pp. 513–520 (2004)
57. Preamthaisong, P., Auyporntrakool, A., Aimtongkham, P., Sriwuttisap, T., So-In, C.: Enhanced DDoS detection using hybrid genetic algorithm and decision tree for SDN. In: 2019 16th International Joint Conference on Computer Science and Software Engineering (JCSSE), pp. 152–157. IEEE (2019)
58. Tavallaee, M., Bagheri, E., Lu, W., Ghorbani, A.A.: A detailed analysis of the KDD CUP 99 data set. In: 2009 IEEE Symposium on Computational Intelligence for Security and Defense Applications, pp. 1–6. IEEE (2009)
59. Chetouane, A., Mabrouk, S., Jemili, I., Mosbah, M.: Vision-based vehicle detection for road traffic congestion classification. Concurr. Comput. Pract. Exp. 34, e5983 (2020)
60. Dong, S., Sarem, M.: DDoS attack detection method based on improved KNN with the degree of DDoS attack in software-defined networks. IEEE Access 8, 5039–5048 (2019)
61. Yuhua, X., Sun, H., Xiang, F., Sun, Z.: Efficient DDoS detection based on K-FKNN in software defined networks. IEEE Access 7, 160536–160545 (2019)
62. Nam, T.M., et al.: Self-organizing map-based approaches in DDoS flooding detection using SDN. In: 2018 International Conference on Information Networking (ICOIN), pp. 249–254. IEEE (2018)
63. Najafabadi, M.M., Villanustre, F., Khoshgoftaar, T.M., Seliya, N., Wald, R., Muharemagic, E.: Deep learning applications and challenges in big data analytics. J. Big Data 2(1), 1–21 (2015)
64. Yegnanarayana, B.: Artificial Neural Networks. PHI Learning Pvt. Ltd. (2009)
65. Hannache, O., Batouche, M.C.: Neural network-based approach for detection and mitigation of DDoS attacks in SDN environments. Int. J. Inf. Secur. Priv. 14(3), 50–71 (2020)
66. Liu, Z., He, Y., Wang, W., Zhang, B.: DDoS attack detection scheme based on entropy and PSO-BP neural network in SDN. Chin. Commun. 16(7), 144–155 (2019)
67. Liu, G., Bao, H., Han, B.: A stacked autoencoder-based deep neural network for achieving gearbox fault diagnosis. Math. Probl. Eng. 2018 (2018)

68. Niyaz, Q., Sun, W., Javaid, A.Y.: A deep learning based DDoS detection system in software-defined networking (SDN). arXiv preprint arXiv:1611.07400 (2016)

69. Ujjan, R.M.A., Pervez, Z., Dahal, K., Bashir, A.K., Mumtaz, R., González, J.: Towards sFlow and adaptive polling sampling for deep learning based DDoS detection in SDN. Fut. Gener. Comput. Syst. **111**, 763–779 (2020)

70. Polat, H., Turkoglu, M., Polat, O.: Deep network approach with stacked sparse autoencoders in detection of DDoS attacks on SDN-based VANET. IET Commun. **14**(22), 4089–4100 (2021)

71. Ahuja, N., Singal, G., Mukhopadhyay, D.: DLSDN: deep learning for DDoS attack detection in software defined networking. In: 2021 11th International Conference on Cloud Computing, Data Science & Engineering (Confluence), pp. 683–688. IEEE (2021)

72. Bapiyev, I.M., Aitchanov, B.H., Tereikovskyi, I.A., Tereikovska, L.A., Korchenko, A.A.: Deep neural networks in cyber attack detection systems. Int. J. Civ. Eng. Technol. (IJCIET) **8**(11), 1086–1092 (2017)

73. Makuvaza, A., Jat, D.S., Gamundani, A.M.: Deep neural network (DNN) solution for real-time detection of distributed denial of service (DDoS) attacks in software defined networks (SDNs). SN Comput. Sci. **2**(2), 1–10 (2021)

74. Wu, Y., Wei, D., Feng, J.: Network attacks detection methods based on deep learning techniques: a survey. Secur. Commun. Netw. **2020** (2020)

75. Nugraha, B., Murthy, R.N.: Deep learning-based slow DDoS attack detection in SDN-based networks. In: 2020 IEEE Conference on Network Function Virtualization and Software Defined Networks (NFV-SDN), pp. 51–56. IEEE (2020)

76. Haider, S.: A deep CNN ensemble framework for efficient DDoS attack detection in software defined networks. IEE Access **8**, 53972–53983 (2020)

77. Tang, T.A., Mhamdi, L., McLernon, D., Zaidi, S.A.R., Ghogho, M.: Deep recurrent neural network for intrusion detection in SDN-based networks. In: 2018 4th IEEE Conference on Network Softwarization and Workshops (NetSoft), pp. 202–206. IEEE (2018)

78. Elsayed, M.S., Le-Khac, N.-A., Dev, S., Jurcut, A.D.: DDoSNET: a deep-learning model for detecting network attacks. In: 2020 IEEE 21st International Symposium on "A World of Wireless, Mobile and Multimedia Networks" (WoWMoM), pp. 391–396. IEEE (2020)

79. Li, C., et al.: Detection and defense of DDoS attack-based on deep learning in OpenFlow-based SDN. Int. J. Commun. Syst. **31**(5), e3497 (2018)

80. Sun, W., Li, Y., Guan, S.: An improved method of DDoS attack detection for controller of SDN. In: 2019 IEEE 2nd International Conference on Computer and Communication Engineering Technology (CCET), pp. 249–253. IEEE (2019)

81. Gupta, B.B., Joshi, R.C., Misra, M.: Defending against distributed denial of service attacks: issues and challenges. Inf. Secur. J. Glob. Perspect. **18**(5), 224–247 (2009)

82. Cai, K.-Y., Wen, C.-Y., Zhang, M.-L.: A critical review on software reliability modeling. Reliab. Eng. Syst. Saf. **32**(3), 357–371 (1991)

83. Netes, V., Kusakina, M.: Reliability challenges in software defined networking. In: Conference of Open Innovations Association, FRUCT 24, pp. 704–709. FRUCT Oy (2019)

84. Eliyan, L.F., Di Pietro, R.: DoS and DDoS attacks in software defined networks: a survey of existing solutions and research challenges. Fut. Gener. Comput. Syst. **122**, 149–171 (2021)

85. Alzahrani, S., Hong, L., et al.: Generation of DDoS attack dataset for effective ids development and evaluation. J. Inf. Secur. **9**(04), 225 (2018)

86. Chandrashekar, G., Sahin, F.: A survey on feature selection methods. Comput. Electr. Eng. **40**(1), 16–28 (2014)
87. Xue, M., Yuan, C., Heyi, W., Zhang, Y., Liu, W.: Machine learning security: threats, countermeasures, and evaluations. IEEE Access **8**, 74720–74742 (2020)

Author Index

Printed in the United States
by Baker & Taylor Publisher Services